The Architecture of Ethics

C000128203

Ethics is one of the most important and least understood aspects of design practice. In his latest book, Thomas Fisher shows how ethics are inherent to the making of architecture – and how architecture offers an unusual and useful way of looking at ethics.

The Architecture of Ethics helps students in architecture and other design disciplines to understand the major approaches to ethics and to apply them to the daily challenges they face in their work. The book covers each of the four dominant approaches to ethics: virtue ethics, social contract ethics, duty ethics, and utilitarian ethics. Each chapter examines the dilemmas designers face from the perspective of one of these categories. Written in an accessible, jargon-free style, the text also features 100 illustrations to help integrate these concepts into the design process and to support visual understanding.

Ethics is now a required part of accredited architecture programs, making this book essential reading for all students in architecture and design.

Thomas Fisher is a Professor in the School of Architecture, Director of the Minnesota Design Center, and former Dean of the College of Design at the University of Minnesota in Minneapolis. He was previously the Editorial Director of *Progressive Architecture* magazine and has written nine books, over 50 book chapters or introductions and over 400 articles in professional journals and major publications. This is the third book he has written about architecture and ethics.

The Architecture of Ethics

Thomas Fisher

 Routledge
Taylor & Francis Group

LONDON AND NEW YORK

First published 2019
by Routledge
2 Park Square, Milton Park, Abingdon, Oxon OX14 4RN

and by Routledge
711 Third Avenue, New York, NY 10017

Routledge is an imprint of the Taylor & Francis Group, an informa business

British Library Cataloguing-in-Publication Data
A catalogue record for this book is available from the British Library

Library of Congress Cataloging-in-Publication Data
Names: Fisher, Thomas, 1953- author.
Title: The architecture of ethics / Thomas Fisher.
Description: New York : Routledge, 2019. | Includes bibliographical
    references and index.
Identifiers: LCCN 2018028643| ISBN 9781138479432
    (hb : alk. paper) | ISBN 9781138479449 (pb : alk. paper) |
    ISBN 9781351065740 (ebook)
Subjects: LCSH: Architects—Professional ethics. | Architectural
    practice—Moral and ethical aspects.
Classification: LCC NA1995 .F565 2019 | DDC 720.92—dc23
LC record available at https://lccn.loc.gov/2018028643

ISBN: 978-1-138-47943-2 (hbk)
ISBN: 978-1-138-47944-9 (pbk)
ISBN: 978-1-351-06574-0 (ebk)

Typeset in Sabon
by Swales & Willis Ltd, Exeter, Devon, UK

Printed in the United Kingdom
by Henry Ling Limited

To my wife and family, without whom I would not have had the time to complete this book

To my students and colleagues, from whom I have learned a lot about life's ethical dilemmas

To my readers, for whom I wrote this book in hopes of piquing interest in architectural ethics

Credits statement

Contents

Illustrations

Photo credits

Table

Introduction

Ethics has dominated the news in recent years, in part because of the challenges to the very idea of ethics that we have seen from some of the world's leaders. Ethics assumes that, based on the facts of a situation, reasonable people can come to some agreement as to what is right or wrong, but when that determination becomes whatever the person or regime in power says is right or wrong and when they dismiss ethics if it gets in the way of whatever they want to do, usually in their personal interest, then ethics seems, if not irrelevant, at least severely embattled. Once a society loses any sense of right or wrong or any ability to come to agreement about it, it devolves into what Thomas Hobbes envisioned as a state of nature "where every man is enemy to every man" and life becomes "solitary, poor, nasty, brutish, and short" (Hobbes, 1910, p.405). Hobbes argued that, to counter this, we needed strong leaders and powerful authorities – a "Leviathan" as he called it. But the challenges to ethics have come from just such figures – Recep Tayyip Erdogan, Vladimir Putin, Bashar al-Assad, Kim Jong-un, Donald Trump – for whom ethics seem like just a nuisance, getting in the way of their assertion of power.

Which makes understanding and valuing ethics more important now than ever before. As I will argue in this book, architecture has something to offer in that effort, in part because some of the most unethical behavior of some of the above leaders has its foundations in the built environment. When Erdogan ordered the commercial redevelopment of Gezi Park, one of the last green spaces in central Istanbul, with no public input or debate, it sparked unrest that later fed a coup attempt, which Erdogan used to crack down on his political enemies. And when Trump faced paying architects who designed some of the buildings he developed before becoming the US president, he sometimes decided he would offer a fraction of what he acknowledged he owed them, threatening to tie things up in court for a very long time if his architects didn't accept his offer. For people like Erdogan and Trump, ethics seems to be whatever they can get away with, and right and wrong, whatever they determine it to be.

If some world leaders care so little about ethics, why should anyone else? Because, in civics as in physics, every action seems to lead to an equal

Figure 0.1 Donald Trump shows why architecture and ethics matter. They are not about creating monuments to one's self or one's own interests, but instead about understanding the world from the point-of-view of others, valuing those perspectives, and accommodating those needs.

and opposite reaction. Ethics has prompted some of the most important and powerful cultural shifts in recent years, from the "Black Lives Matter" movement, in which people of all colors have demanded an end to police violence, to the "Occupy Wall Street" movement, with people protesting the outrageous economic inequality in the US and around the world, to the "Me Too" movement, where women (and men) subjected to sexual assault have brought down powerful men who thought that they could get away with such behavior. These movements have arisen out of an empathetic under-standing of what it feels like to be abused, oppressed, and even murdered by people in power, and from a refusal to tolerate such behavior, regardless of the consequences.

The built environment, again, has played a supporting role in these ethi-cally driven movements. The video capture of police gunning down black people has almost all occurred in the public places such as streets or parks, highlighting the danger that many people of color feel in their own neighbor-hoods, not just from criminals but also from law enforcement. The occu-pation of lower Manhattan's Zuccotti Park during the Occupy Wall Street movement highlighted the importance of public spaces in these protests. Meanwhile, the sexual harassment that propelled the Me Too movement, has almost always happened in private places – offices, hotel rooms, apartments – which have become equally contested spaces between those who wield financial and political power and their victims, who increasingly overpower them in the court of public opinion. Which is where the power of ethics lies. When a person engaged in unethical behavior gets "outed" and the behavior widely known, the loss of reputation ends careers and makes it almost impossible for that person to ever recoup – something that applies to professionals as much as it does to politicians, police, and movie producers.

Ethics, then, becomes a way to protect oneself by respecting others. It becomes a way of seeing things from the perspective of those most affected by our decisions and of taking into account their interests and needs in every action we take. Those who have never learned the value of ethics may see such a mindset creating "suckers" or "losers," two of Donald Trump's favorite dismissals, but such self-declared winners ultimately lose big time, when no one wants to work with them, be with them, or even help them when they might need it. As the above movements show, empathy has its limits, and the line gets drawn with those who have willfully abused others and acted unethically for so long. To all the unscrupulous leaders, avaricious investors, and sexually harassing men whose reputations seem destined for ruin, good riddance.

While we often think of ethics applying to our individual actions, our notions of right and wrong or good and bad relate just as much to the larger economic and political forces that shape and constrain the designed world in which we live. In that sense, designers literally give physical form to the public policies that politicians have put in place, even though many designers rarely think of what we do in this way. We tend to judge a design according to its aesthetics and pragmatics: does it look good, function well, and meet our budget? But we also need to assess a design in terms of the ethics of the codes and regulations, taxes and fees, and incentives and inducements that influenced the designer's decisions and that defined the context within which the design evolved.

We may not talk as much about the latter because public policies can sometimes seem more like a force of nature and something beyond our control, but those policies actually arise out of a kind of design thinking. As designers do every day, elected officials devise policies in order to achieve a desired end or to address an unmet need, and the designed products and environments that literally embed those policies in their form, function, and material, provide one of the best ways of judging the merit of these policies. What we design mirrors what we value as individuals and as a political and economic community.

We enact that community through a mixture of carrots and sticks. The social contract of most modern countries accepts the use of incentives as well as prohibitions and penalties in order to achieve what at least those in power at any given moment conceive of as good or bad. And the differing degree to which those in power use such means depends upon their approach to ethics. Those who favor incentivizing good behavior, for example, implicitly embrace virtue ethics. If we believe almost all people have the capacity to be virtuous – honest, fair, prudent, and so on – then incentivizing people with economic carrots makes total sense.

Meanwhile, decision-makers who have a less sanguine view of human nature may resort more to sticks. Utilitarian ethics often underpins public policies that use the "stick" of taxation or fees. Such policies rarely prohibit certain behaviors or decisions, but instead focus on spreading resources in order to benefit the greatest number and on nudging people toward seeing their own self-interest in the common good. Likewise, deontological ethics, based on his belief that there exist absolute and universal rights and wrongs, can lead politicians to enact laws that wield a big stick, proscribing certain behaviors or prohibiting the use of certain substances or materials. Drawing such a clear line between the legal and illegal echoes Immanuel Kant's advice to not do anything that we wouldn't accept if universally applied (Kant, 2016).

Architects do not just respond to these carrots and sticks; professionals also reinforce them through what gets designed, and the more we attend to the ethics of design, the more conscious we will be of the values embedded in what gets made and built. In an era of global awareness and increasing diversity of all sorts, ethics has moved away from a big-systems approach to moral dilemmas, in which everything gets measured according to single criteria and has moved instead toward the contextually responsive, situationally sensitive, empathetically grounded actions that may be very different from one place to another. As the social psychologist Jonathan Haidt has argued, most cultures share a sense of the importance of ethics in human interactions, but cultures vary widely in terms for what they emphasize and prioritize in terms of morals, and understanding that and resisting the imposition of one cultural norm on another has become a key part of what constitutes ethics in the twenty-first century (Haidt, 2012).

The architecture community has had to learn this, sometimes the hard way. Possibly because buildings involve systems – mechanical systems, plumbing systems, and so on – architects have seemed particularly attracted to big, systemic, ethical ideas. Modern architecture, for example, had roots in both the utilitarianism of nineteenth-century England and the idealism of nineteenth-century Germany, especially that of Hegel. While buildings all have specific contexts in which they stand, many modernists embraced – perhaps unknowingly – Hegel's idea that history moves forward through visionary individuals who have helped us march toward greater freedom for more and more people. These "world-historical figures," as Hegel called them, who defined the zeitgeist or the spirit of each age, bring to mind the so-called masters of modern architecture, people such as Le Corbusier, Frank Lloyd Wright, and Mies van der Rohe, whose use of the "free plan" seemed to embody the Hegelian ideal of maximizing human freedom and whose interest in new technology seemed to define the zeitgeist (Hegel, 2001).

Architecture and ethics, though, do not always align. The idealism and utilitarianism that characterized modern architecture in the early twentieth century ran counter to a growing skepticism about ethics in Anglo-American philosophy. Ethics came to be seen by many as a subjective or "emotive" expression of personal preferences, lacking the clarity or objectivity of linguistic or logical analysis. As C. L. Stevenson, for instance, argued in his 1944 book *Ethics and Language*, we have to distinguish between beliefs based on facts, which can be mandated, and attitudes toward behaviors, which should remain advisory (Stevenson, 1944). The skepticism and scientism that came to characterize aspects of twentieth-century ethics eventually influenced architecture, as many post-World War II buildings became exercises in technical efficiency and the mass production of repetitive elements – an architecture of facts rather than behavior.

Not all twentieth-century philosophers dismissed ethics as subjective. The ethics of John Dewey, for example, had an enormous influence on education in North America, above all his "laboratory method" of experimentation as a way of resolving moral as well as social and political dilemmas (Dewey, 1939). Dewey's ethics, at once progressive and pragmatic, paralleled the belief of many design educators that design studio should be less a place of pupilage and more a laboratory for the exploration of new ideas. By the 1960s, this belief in the value of experimentation took more radical forms. Just as Karl Marx's ethical materialism had turned G.W.F. Hegel's ethical idealism on its head, so a growing number of architecture students and faculty in the 1960s overturned the Hegelian idealization of the modern masters and modern technology to embrace a more Marxist interest in the needs of the working class and the poor (Marx, 2009). Meanwhile, the emerging youth culture of the era reflected an ethics that was at once nihilistic and idealistic: Nietzschean in its confrontation with power and Rousseauian in its yearning to return to a state of nature.

By the end of the twentieth century, both architecture and ethics had entered a postmodern period of revivals. The resurgence of interest among educators and practitioners in architectural history, for example, paralleled a revived interest among philosophers in historical approaches to ethics. John Rawls's argument about the need to attend to the needs of the least advantaged members of society prompted a revival among philosophers of the social contract ethics that had last flourished in the seventeenth and eighteenth centuries (Rawls, 1971). Similarly, in architecture, the rise of participatory planning and protests by historic preservationists against urban renewal had strong repercussions in architecture schools during the 1970s and reflected a like commitment to questions related to the architect's "social contract" with the public.

A revival of other philosophical traditions with ethical implications also emerged in the 1970s and 1980s, two of which had great influence on architecture education. The first, phenomenology, derived from the work of philosophers such as Maurice Merleau-Ponty, who linked both architecture and ethics back to the latter's Greek root word, *ethos*, meaning "accustomed place" (Merleau-Ponty, 2004). The embrace of phenomenology also reflected a revival of the pre-Socratic philosophers' focus on the existential meanings of the material world. A new focus on experiential qualities and particularities of places, which became a central focus of architectural and urban design education in many schools, showed the influence of phenomenology and existential ethics that continues to this day.

A second philosophy with roots in an ancient tradition of moral analysis, virtue ethics, also witnessed a revival in the work of a number of philosophers, many of them women – Elizabeth Anscombe, Susan Wolf, Iris Murdoch, and Philippa Foot, among others (Berges, 2015). Their questioning of the rigidity and absolutism of modern utilitarian ethics led to a more modest, contextual, and character-based approach to morality. Within architecture schools, such an approach translated into a new interest in the context and character of buildings and to questions of who gets left out of decision making and public discourse – a sensibility that also remains very much in force today.

Postmodernism led to new understandings of architects' ethical responsibilities as well. The ethics of care that emerged in the 1980s in the work of feminist philosophers such as Carol Gilligan and Nel Noddings resonated with the thinking of many architecture educators, who had become increasingly critical of the repressive qualities of the built environment and the need for more diverse and flexible ways of accommodating people's lives (Gilligan, 1982). The incursion of feminist ethics into a once male-dominated field like architecture has also had consequences for the quality of life in many schools, making them less like fraternity houses and more open to a plurality of student backgrounds and values.

Finally, postmodern revisions of ethical philosophy contributed to an expansion of architecture's purview beyond its traditional subject – human beings – to embrace the good of other species and the planet as a whole. Thinkers such as Arne Naess, Peter Singer, and Bill McKibben enlarged architects' sense of obligation to ecosystems and the deep interconnections existing among the parts of "one world," to use Singer's term (Singer, 2002). The growing number of sustainability programs in architecture schools and the addition of an environmental canon to the AIA's code of ethics give evidence of the widening influence of environmental ethics.

Faced with ongoing environmental damage, an exponential increase in human population, rapid depletion of finite resources, and extinction of irreplaceable species, architects may find ethics a useful way of sorting out the appropriate responses to these challenges. And in so doing, we may come back around to the utilitarianism that prompted modernism to begin with. When we include all people, all species, and future generations in our calculus of the greatest good for the greatest number, we may see an architectural profession that looks less at one-off custom design solutions and more at how we can help conserve energy, steward natural resources, serve the needs of billions of ill-housed people, and preserve the habitat of other species upon whose survival humankind depends.

That expansion of who and what architects care about has led to an ethical turn in the profession. Now a required part of architectural education and a frequent topic at architectural conferences, ethics has become an integral part not just of architectural practice, but also of how we think about and go about designing the built environment. In some sense, the early modernist architects would have agreed. Ethics mattered to them too, but the big-system ethics they largely embraced represented Western hegemony and led to the imposition of idealized forms on people and places in completely inappropriate ways. Like one of the grand ethical systems that argued for one way of determining right and wrong, these grand architectural statements paid little or no attention to cultural or climatic differences and seemed to assume that the Western model represented a universal solution, an International Style, that all others would embrace and the only rational way to live.

The ethical turn in twenty-first-century architecture starts from a very different place. It holds that the people most affected by architects' decisions and actions need to be engaged and active participants in the design process, which begins with an empathetic understanding of diverse perspective and a respect for cultural and climatic differences. In this way, architecture becomes a way of manifesting, in physical form, people's ideas of what constitutes a good life. Every design communicates those values and every design decision has ethical implications as a result. Of course, like many of the aesthetic and pragmatic judgements designers make, ethical ones may be more intuitive or inherited than conscious: we know that families have gradations of more public and more private spaces in their homes or that teachers and students, judges and juries, musicians and audiences all have certain spatial relationships that reflect long-held traditions and that change slowly. Recognizing those traditions, assessing those changes, and respecting those relationships – while also questioning, challenging, and exploring alternatives to them – represents one of the key roles that architects play and one of the most important values that the profession brings to a society.

This book follows that path. It does not advocate a particular ethical position or posit some grand moral system, but instead reflects the diverse ways in which ethics can help us understand the dilemmas that architects face in the course of practice and in the design of the built environment. The following essays take a pragmatic view that ethics has to be useful and offer relevant guidance to architects who are constantly confronted by trade-offs

Table 0.1 Ethics types

	Individual	Group
Character	**Virtue ethics** Addressing the character of a professional and of a building in terms of form and features	**Social Contract ethics** Dealing with our societal obligations and the content and context of a building
Actions	**Deontological (Duty) ethics** Involving our responsibility as a professional and that of a building via its meaning and purpose	**Utilitarian ethics** Looking at the effect of our actions and our work on the greatest number of others

in their work and who have to make decisions that have an impact on the people who build and occupy their buildings.

Ethics has a long history, but it might be helpful for those who have never studied the field to see it in terms of four basic approaches having to do with the focus of ethical considerations – on our character or our actions – and with the scale of ethical considerations – the individual or the group. We might organize these in a table, each quadrant of which represents a major area of ethical thought and its relationship to architectural practice:

Embedded in these four approaches to ethics lies the very definition of an architect, as a licensed professional responsible to protect the health, safety, and welfare of those who use or are affected by their buildings.

Virtue ethics

The very idea of a "professional" brings with it certain personal character-istics or behaviors that include being fair in one's assessment of situations, judicious in making decisions, temperate in one's responses, courageous enough to do the right thing, honest in one's dealings with others, empa-thetic toward the needs of others, and so on. In ethics, we call those virtues, and this approach, which dates back to the ancient Greeks, focuses on the development and deployment of a good character.

Social contract ethics

Licensure also represents a contract with society, which grants professionals a monopoly in the marketplace in exchange for our looking after the public good. This especially applies to the profession of architecture, which gives form to the public realm and helps define the public good in ways that many other fields do not. While our social contract can have a variety of interpretations – should the architect reinforce social conventions, for example, or challenge them in order to free us from tradition? – there remains a professional obligation that extends beyond the interests of the clients who pay our fees to others in the larger society who do not have the ability to pay and yet who also feel the effect of what architects do.

Deontological or duty ethics

Professional activities are inherently ethical, as well, in that they involve our duty to others; even where we don't have a legal obligation or a social expectation to act in a certain way, professionals often have an ethical responsibility to take into account the needs not just of those who inhabit buildings, but also of those affected directly or indirectly by our decisions, such as future inhabitants of a building, those visiting it or passing by, those involved in the manufacture of materials and products used in the building, and even other species whose habitat may have been altered by it in some way.

Utilitarian ethics

Finally, the architect's obligation to protect health, safety, and welfare take us far beyond the important and yet narrow requirement that a building accommodate a client's program, that it not fall down and harm people, and that it not negatively affect the health of those who inhabit it. The broad categories of health, safety, and welfare, by their very nature, involve architects in the utilitarian ethic of trying to achieve the greatest good for the greatest number. The architect cannot protect the health or safety of the users of a building, for example, if the structure harms that of those occupying neighboring properties. If anything, professional ethics requires that architects take into account the public's health, safety, and welfare and not just that of clients.

Those four approaches, in other words, remain fundamental to architecture and to what architects do: providing us with ways of assessing the merits of a design:

- Does the design have the right character given its context? (virtue ethics)
- Does it enhance the good of a place and of those who use it? (contract ethics)
- Does it do the right thing despite potentially negative consequences? (duty ethics)
- Does it achieve the greatest good for the greatest number? (utilitarian ethics)

As the essays in this book try to show, ethics is an inseparable part of the built environment, as essential to its creation as the bricks and mortar with which buildings are made. Ethics also provides a diverse and varied landscape of issues and ideas that weave through the pieces in this book. Each essay here can stand on its own and you can read each one in whatever order suits you, which explains their alphabetical arrangement, although many of the chapters follow on each other and so reading this book from front to back will also pay dividends. Ethics and architecture remain endlessly fascinating and highly intertwined fields, and I hope, after reading this book, that you find yourself as caught up in their complex relationship as I have been and that you, too, feel inclined to want to explore the ways in which each deepens our understanding of the other.

References

Berges, Sandrine. 2015. *A Feminist Perspective on Virtue Ethics*. London: Palgrave Macmillan.

Dewey, John. 1939. *Intelligence in the Modern World: John Dewey's Philosophy*. New York: The Modern Library.

Gilligan, Carol. 1982. *In A Different Voice*. Cambridge: Harvard University Press.

Haidt, Jonathan. 2012. *The Righteous Mind: Why Good People are Divided by Politics and Religion*. New York: Random House.

Hegel, Georg Wilhelm Friedrich. 2001. *The Philosophy of History*. Kitchener, Ontario: Batoche Books. http://www.efm.bris.ac.uk/het/hegel/history.pdf

Hobbes, Thomas. 1910. *Of Man, Being the First Part of Leviathan*. The Harvard Classics, Vol. 34. Cambridge: Harvard University Press.

Kant, Immanuel. 2016. *The Collected Works of Immanuel Kant*. London: Delphi Classics.

Marx, Karl. 2009. *Das Kapital*. Washington DC: Regnery Publishing.

Merleau-Ponty, Maurice. 2004. Baldwin, Thomas, ed. *Maurice Merleau-Ponty: Basic Writings*. New York: Routledge.

Rawls, John. 1971. *A Theory of Justice*. Cambridge: Belknap Press of Harvard University Press.

Singer, Peter. 2002. *One World: The Ethics of Globalization*. New Haven: Yale University Press.

Stevenson, C. L. 1944. *Ethics and Language*. New Haven: Yale University Press

Chapter 1

Breaking rules

I grew up in the 1960s and often heard people say that "Rules are meant to be broken." That idea appealed to my rebellious teenager mind, but as I have thought about it since, the phrase seems much more complex and much less evident. What rules? Made by whom? For what reason? And why are they "meant" to be broken? Broken by whom, in which situations? Those questions raise all sorts of ethical quandaries and they lie at the heart of architecture, the field I have pursued since becoming an adult.

Creative people, of course, have always broken rules; societies move forward when some have the insight to see a new and better way to do something and the courage to act on those ideas, regardless of what the rules allow. Indeed, the most important innovations make the old rules seem absurd and almost impossible to return to, even if we chose. But something changed in many Western societies after World War II. Breaking the rules became not something for the exceptional few, but something that became the norm and almost expected of us, wisely or not.

I saw this in my own education. My architect grandfather, Harold Fisher, trained in the methods of the École des Beaux Arts, saw our field as one of applying well-established rules to new situations. He did not question the validity of the rules and he saw the creative act in terms of how well he chose which rules to use. My architect professors urged the opposite. For them, the originality of our work as students and the unprecedented and even uncanny nature of what we produced marked the difference between the ordinary and extraordinary projects – the B and C grades versus the As.

The same has characterized the architecture of our time. The architectural media cannot get enough of rule-breaking work, as I saw in the years that I worked as a magazine editor. If architects did too many buildings too much alike, magazines like mine seemed to tire of them and look for new people to publish, as if practitioners not only had to the break the received rules of our field, but also their own rules, which had governed their previous production. Originality reigned and it required continuous renewal or the architect no longer seemed original.

That also seemed to work when pursuing commissions. I once served on the architect-selection committee for a major museum project, which

Figure 1.1 My grandfather was hired just before the Crash of 1929 by architect Bertram
Goodhue, the architect of St. Thomas Church in New York City, who, like
many of his generation, saw architecture as an evolutionary development of
traditional forms.

required that the architects come to the interview to talk about their relevant
experience and qualifications for the project, without any design drawings or
models. All of the architects did as requested, except one, who hand-carried
into the interview a model of what he would design and who subsequently
received the commission (and ended up doing an exceptional building).

I supported the client's request that architects not do any design work up
front since in minimized the uncompensated work of the firms competing
for the commission, and the museum director liked the idea as well, since
he did not want the architect to design the building without the input of
his staff and board members. But that experience made me wonder if rule-
breaking had become almost expected of creative people. When is it acceptable to break the rules and when is it not? Ethics tells us that being good and
doing what is right usually means following the rules, while in aesthetics – at
least in the modern era – those who do the unexpected or the outlandish
seem to succeed. So how do we balance ethics and aesthetics, cooperation
and creativity? The answer to such a question depends, in part, in how we
think about ethics.

Those who measure the ethics of an action according to its consequences
might say that the architect who won the job did the right thing. His decision

to break the rules and bring a model to the interview was a good one, at least for him. And, since he did an exceptional building, his receipt of the commission proved to be a good decision for the client and the people who use the facility. Utilitarian ethics asks that we consider the greatest good for the greatest number, and in that sense, the greatest number – the many users of the building – did receive the greatest benefit with the selection of that architect.

That brings us to another way of thinking about ethics: Immanuel Kant's categorical imperative: that we judge the rightness of an action according to whether or not we would want it to be universal. If we let one person break a rule, Kant would argue, then we have to let everyone break that rule (Kant, 2016). You could argue that every competitor, in this case, was equally free to ignore the request of the selection committee, although that committee did not say that its interview requirements were just a suggestion or that respecting them was voluntary. Which raises the question of where responsibility in this case lies. In society at large, we not only hold people responsible for obeying the law, we also hold officials responsible for enforcing it, and so, by awarding the commission to the architect who ignored their requirement, the selection committee ended up rewarding the very behavior they did not want, which is not a good signal to send at the beginning of an architect-client relationship.

In this case, the architect so impressed the selection committee that they overlooked the very requirements they had imposed. And, because the architect produced an exceptional building, you could argue that it does not matter what happened during the interview. If something ends in great architecture, do the means of getting there really matter? That question echoes the disconnection between aesthetics and ethics that has existed in Western countries for at least a century. Good art comes from good artists, who may or may not be good people, and history offers us plenty of examples of this, of despicable behavior on the part of those who created delightful masterpieces.

Ethics also demands that we make distinctions between unwise actions and illegal or unethical ones. In this case, no one other than the architect himself would have been harmed had his decision to bring a model to the interview backfired on him and led to his disqualification. Which also helps explain why we accept a degree of separation between aesthetics and ethics. A painter who takes an aesthetic risk in a painting does no harm except perhaps to his or her own reputation, and so healthy societies accept and even encourage such violations of the rules in order to realize something new and important.

Not so with ethics, which involves the effect of our actions on others. If that same painter forged a famous painting and passed it off as the original, we would not chalk that up to creativity and excuse it as artists just being artists. A faked painting breaks not an aesthetic rule, but an ethical one and it damages not just the painter's reputation, but also the people who buy or

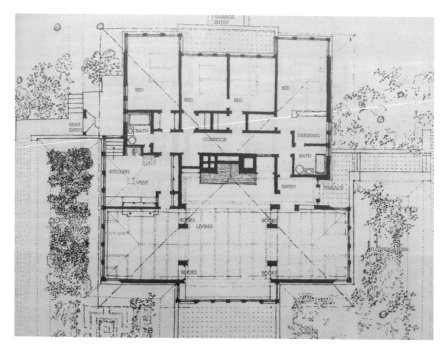

Figure 1.2 Frank Lloyd Wright epitomized the dilemma of the great artist as a not-so-great person. After designing this house for Edwin and Mamah Borthwick Cheney, for example, Wright and Mamah ran away together to Europe.

sell the copy thinking it authentic. Aesthetic rule-breaking may challenge our expectations or change our perceptions, but ethical rule-breaking can harm others and ultimately the ethical violators themselves; we allow that behavior – or look the other way – at our peril.

Reference

Kant, Immanuel. 2016. *The Collected Works of Immanuel Kant*. London: Delphi Classics.

Chapter 2

Built environments

Although the word aesthetics has the letters for the word "ethics" embedded in it, the former has long buried the latter, at least in architecture school, where I quickly learned that pragmatics, physics, and aesthetics seemed to matter most. How a building functions, how it stands up, and what it looks like – its commodity, firmness, and delight – remained the central concerns of us as students, as they have for architects since at least the time of the Roman architect, Vitruvius. In my school, at least, the equally vital questions of ethics rarely got asked, questions such as: what *good* does a building do, for whom, and in what way? The ethical implications of buildings seemed to me then as they do now to be as relevant as function and form, but because few architects ever receive even a basic grounding in ethics, its questions go unanswered, even though they would help us produce a better, more equitable, and more resilient built environment.

This ethical lacuna seems odd since the ethical dilemmas of our lives all happen in physical space, in the interactions of individuals and groups in particular places: in the enclosures in which we live or work, the streets on which we travel, and the landscapes which we enjoy. These places may not cause our behavior, good or bad, but neither do they play a neutral role. The design of an office may make it easier for a boss to hide his sexual harassment of an employee, the location of a community may signal that some people are welcome and others not, and the layout of a city might separate neighborhoods in ways that allow people of different socio-economic levels to never come into contact with each other.

Physical space, in other words, has more than a coincidental relationship to our behavior; it creates the opportunities to do right or wrong and as such, we need to take ethics into account when we design spaces. Most designers, though, don't do this, at least consciously and intentionally. Architectural ethics, for instance, mostly deals with issues of practice and the contractual or professional obligations that architects have to the public, to clients, to colleagues, and to the natural environment. The ethical implications of what architects create – the spaces in which we spend our days – rarely gets discussed and hardly gets mentioned in architects' code of ethics. The same seems true of ethics as a branch of philosophy: space rarely gets mentioned in the ethical literature and ethics has remained largely a-spatial over most of its history, even though ethical dilemmas have a clear spatial aspect.

Take the famous Trolley Problem in ethics. In this thought experiment, a person in control of a train switch has to decide whether to let a run-away trolley kill several railroad workers along one track or to pull the switch to kill one person tied to the other track. That classic ethical dilemma has value in showing how utilitarianism, by seeking the greatest good for the greatest number, can lead to the obviously unethical act of murdering a person, but the Trolley Problem also remains vague about the actual space in which this dilemma occurs. Are the workers on the track within shouting range to warn them of the run-away trolley? Does their freedom of movement – as opposed to that of the person tied to the track – give them more agency and make their fate less determined by the person at the switch? And does their acceptance of an element of danger as track workers make this a story more about an occupational hazard than about an ethical dilemma? (Cathcart, 2013).

The relative neglect of the spatial aspects of ethics and the ethical aspects of space may stem, in part, from the intervention of the law in situations in which conflicts occur in physical environments. We can all think of scenarios

Figure 2.1 Philippa Foot's original 1967 formulation of the Trolley Problem dealt with the ethical dilemma of sacrificing one person to save many rail workers in the way of a runaway train. Judith Thompson's 1976 variation forced us to ask: would we push an innocent bystander off a bridge if that would stop the trolley?

in which spatial conflicts raise contractual or legal issues: of tenants who damage their apartment or office, of property owners who fight over the boundary that separates their land, and of nations that close their borders to immigrants out of prejudice or fear. Such situations often get addressed through arbitration, litigation, or deportation, rather than through ethical debate or spatial design. In one sense, we have come to define space so often in terms of property – who has or hasn't the right to do what where – that we don't always see the connection between space and human agency – what is the meaning of what we do where.

And here, design has a useful and often unrecognized contribution to make. Unlike the law, which encourages us to view conflicts in black or white and property as public or private, design sees the world and its human interactions in more nuanced ways, as shades of gray. While architects and landscape architects, for instance, respect the boundaries between public and private property, their designs also acknowledge that people continually cross those boundaries and that these spaces exist within gradations of public, semi-public, semi-private, and private realms.

Likewise, while the law often frames a situation into a set of right-or-wrong, win-or-lose scenarios, design does the opposite. It seeks ways to enable both sides to win or at least have enough of their concerns addressed to make the situation less adversarial. In response to the scenarios above, a designer might try to design an apartment to minimize the potential for damage, to demarcate more clearly the boundaries between properties, or to accommodate refugees in ways that meet their basic needs. Design, in other words, becomes an anticipatory and precautionary way of addressing spatial conflicts, helping us avoid legal ethical conflicts and to keep us out of court.

But what role has ethics played in the formation of built space? From what we know of how humans lived for most of our history as a species, our ancestors had great ingenuity in making their shelter from what they had at hand and in stewarding the flora and fauna upon which they depended in order to ensure that they had enough for the next season. While homo sapiens clearly had negative effects on the environments, including the extinction of other species and the elimination of competitors, the minimal impact that human shelter had on the ecosystems we occupied also brings to mind the deep ecology ethic of Arne Naess. For most of human history, architecture remained an integral part of the natural environment from which it arose (Naess, 2008).

That changed with the rise of permanent settlements and fixed buildings some 10,000 years ago. With that came the ethical question that preoccupied many of the ancient Greek and Roman philosophers: How should we live? That question had spatial aspects, in the sense that a balanced life needs an equally balanced built environment, and that questioned generated a fairly consistent response up to the modern era, in which a balanced life was reflected in the balanced forms and spaces of Classical architecture, which remained popular in the West into the early twentieth century. It wasn't until people began to see the imbalances behind the Classical facades – the pollution and poverty that an increasingly industrialized world had created – that the misalignment between the aesthetic order of Classicism and ethical disorder that it covered up became intolerable.

Modernism offered a new answer to the question of what constituted a good life. Ethics became not an ideal expressed in the form and facades of Classical buildings, but a negotiation of the diverse interests of people who occupy or are affected by the built environment. No longer about commodity, firmness, and delight, ethics became about health, safety, and welfare – the basis upon which professional licensure now rests. And as a result, the ethics of the built environment became more a matter of politics than of philosophy, more about what community members valued rather than what idealists professed. Which may help explain why ethics largely disappeared from the modern architecture curriculum for much of the last century: as Friedrich Nietzsche argued, ethics seemed to have become about power and architecture, "a sort of oratory of power by means of form" (Nietzsche, 2007, p.69).

Figure 2.2 Nietzsche lived in Basel as well as Turin, where he occupied an apartment in the building at the far right in this photo. Walking across Piazza Carlo Alberto, with its classical buildings and formal landscape, he could see how architecture represented "a kind of oratory of power."

Neglecting to teach ethics does not make ethical conflicts go away, however. Which led to ethics becoming a required part of architectural education by the end of the last century as both professionals and professors started to confront the inequities and injustices embedded in their buildings, the self-serving and self-deluding aspects of their culture, and the contradictions and inconsistencies inherent in their practices. The ethical question of who and what gets left out in the creation of the built environment has helped us recognize how many others rarely get considered in the design process: other generations, other species, and other people and cultures.

This, in turn, has raised questions about the ethics of a practice model in which designers largely focus on the needs of the clients paying their fees and of a regulatory model in which physical safety becomes the dominant concern, with little or no attention given to the health or welfare of the larger community. Architects are like the person at that switch in the Trolley Problem, faced with the dilemma of saving our client tied to the architectural track or saving the many people affected by our actions. A spatial approach to this ethical conundrum suggests that it doesn't have to be either-or and that, instead of our having to choose between one or many, we can design situations that create better options for all.

References

Cathcart, Thomas. 2013. *The Trolley Problem, or Would You Throw the Fat Guy off the Bridge? A Philosophical Conundrum*. New York: Workman.

Naess, Arne. 2008. *The Ecology of Wisdom: Writings by Arne Naess*. Berkeley: Counterpoint.

Nietzsche, Friedrich. 2007. *Twilight of the Idols*. Hertfordshire, England: Wordsworth.

Chapter 3

Capitalism

Capitalism has the potential to create better options and expand opportunities for all, but it too often fails to do so for all but a relatively few. When a lawyer colleague of mine, Stephen Young, wrote a book about this, called *Moral Capitalism*, I thought his book's title constituted a non-sequitur (Young, 2003). Capitalism seemed, especially of late, at once immoral, in terms of the harm to the planet that it continues to cause, and amoral, in the sense that so many of its beneficiaries seem indifferent to its negative impacts. If capitalism has a moral sense these days, it seems to lie to the moral of Donald Trump, when he says that you can't be too greedy.

Capitalism, though, didn't start that way. The first and in some ways still, the most insightful proponent of capitalism – Adam Smith – taught moral philosophy at the University of Glasgow and he thought that marketplace economies depend upon what he called "moral sentiments," in which we imagine ourselves in the position of others less advantaged than ourselves (Smith, 2011). Successful companies do this all the time: they understand the customer well enough to ensure that their products and services meet that person's needs and their suppliers well enough to have good relationships and fair prices. But Smith also thought capitalists have an obligation to the general public. Living in an era of small shopkeepers and local production, he saw scale as a brake on greedy or amoral behavior, recognizing that it is not in our self-interest to pollute the air that we also breathe or the water that we also drink.

The problem occurs when capitalism goes global. Without physical proximity and a connection to the people most affected by their actions, global capitalists have few constraints on their greed as long as they turn a profit for their shareholders and meet at least the minimum requirements for worker safety and satisfaction. If they pollute the air and water in some far away country or engage in exploitative practices in some poorly policed place, they face few negatives consequences and potentially a lot more profit. Smith would have hated such capitalism and would have likely seen it as an amoral version of what he envisioned. He mocked, for instance, those who care too much for what he called the baubles of wealth, urging that we

Figure 3.1 Although considered the "father" of capitalism, Adam Smith taught moral philosophy at the University of Glasgow and understood the value of public investments and the public good to balance the pursuit of profit.

instead create an economy in which the Invisible Hand of the marketplace raises everyone's fortunes, not just those of a few (Smith, 1994).

Architecture occupies an interesting and awkward place in that tension between local and global capitalism. On one hand, architecture is always local, involving the construction of buildings fixed in particular places, built mostly by people who work there and used mostly by people who live there. In that sense, it represents a huge force in enacting Smith's idea of moral sentiment, where a building's owners and occupants would not want it to degrade the environment that they use every day. Such moral sentiments become evident every time community members register their opinions about buildings going up in their neighborhoods, worried about the impact of more people, cars, and congestion or about the shadows cast, energy required, or space used by the new structure. Architects and clients may not like the pushback they sometimes encounter when they present a new design to a community, but this is the marketplace working as it should, with the invisible hand of moral sentiment keeping capitalism within the constraints that people see as constituting a larger, public good.

On the other hand, architecture has gone global. Architects now do work all over the world for many of their corporate and wealthiest institutional and individual clients, and there exist far fewer constraints in some, less-developed countries in terms of what a building looks like, how big it can be, where it goes, or what environmental impact it has. Just as capitalists living far away feel few of the negative consequences of their decisions and feel free to do what they could not get away with in their home country, so too can architects, within the limits of international building codes and local regulations, get away with a lot without much pushback from communities in which they build.

The late architect, Zaha Hadid, faced this issue when asked about the many migrant workers who have died in Qatar, where she had designed a major project. She rightly observed that she, as an architect, has "nothing to do with the workers" and that the mistreatment of construction workers is "an issue the government – if there's a problem – should pick up. Hopefully, these things will be resolved." (Goldberger, 2014) While she may have been unfairly blamed for implying that she didn't care about the working conditions of construction crews, the reaction to her comment shows the extent of the public concern about potentially exploitative behavior on the part of global enterprises, be they multi-national corporations or internationally known architects.

Such cases suggest that moral sentiment can exist at a global level, if only through the leveraging of public opinion via the media. Hadid's filing of a defamation suit against the writer who most vocally criticized her remarks, like Trump's lambasting the media and calling any coverage he doesn't like fake news, shows how much global capitalism doesn't like any challenge to its power and prerogative. But too bad. If we have any hope of achieving Smith's original idea of a morally grounded capitalism, then the people who have profited enormously from it – architects and clients alike – need to expect pushback and respect constraints.

Hadid's architecture also may help explain why global capitalism so resists such constraints. The nineteenth-century philosopher Friedrich Nietzsche saw the world cycling between periods of order and disorder, calmness and wildness, or as Nietzsche put it, between the Apollonian, referring to Apollo, the Greek god of reason and truth, and the Dionysian, referring to Dionysus, the Greek god of wine and ecstasy (Nietzsche, 1994). That idea echoed the notion of the eighteenth-century writer, Edmund Burke, that the West has embraced two opposite ways of thinking about aesthetics, as either a search for beauty or the "sublime" (Burke, 2001) We sometimes admire the orderliness, proportion, and balance that have traditionally characterized beauty, said Burke, and at other times, we like the messy, disturbing, and overpowering nature of the sublime.

Hadid's buildings, with their sinuous forms and scale-less shapes that look like animals about to swallow all who enter, exemplify the Dionysian sublime. That sublimity has come to characterize much of what global capitalism produces, going to ever greater extremes in order to garner publicity, gain an advantage, or generate faster growth, whether it be with an

Figure 3.2 Zaha Hadid's Messner Mountain Museum Corones focuses on mountaineering and it captures in its cantilevered forms and projecting terrace the daring and vertiginous activity of climbing mountains, embodying the architectural sublime.

attention-getting building that gulps down its occupants or a profit-seeking conglomerate that devours its competitors.

If any consolation exists, it is that both Burke and Nietzsche recognized that cultures eventually tire of the sublime and cycle back to more restrained, Apollonian behavior. As we have begun to see among a younger generation who, like many of my students, see the architecture of someone like Zaha Hadid as more indulgent than inspiring. This generation seems to recognize the Dionysian mess that it has inherited from previous generations, as a growing number of people – young and old – increasingly favoring conservation rather than waste, environmental and social concern rather than artistic excess and personal expression. Maybe, just maybe, moral capitalism will once again prevail.

References

Burke, Edmund. 2001. *A Philosophical Inquiry into the Origin of our Ideas of the Sublime and Beautiful*. Harvard Classics, Vol. 24, Part 2. New York: Bartleby.

Goldberger, Paul. 2014. "Zaha Hadid is still Wrong about Construction Worker Conditions," *Vanity Fair*. August. New York: Condé Nast. www.vanityfair.com/

culture/architecture/2014/08/zaha-hadid-worker-conditions-lawsuit. Accessed July 31, 2018.

Nietzsche, Friedrich. 1994. *The Birth of Tragedy*. New York: Penguin.

Smith, Adam. 2011. *The Theory of Moral Sentiments*. New York: Gutenberg.

Smith, Adam. 1994. *The Wealth of Nations*. New York: Random House.

Young, Stephen. 2003. *Moral Capitalism: Reconciling Private Interest with the Public Good*. San Francisco: Berrett-Koehler.

Chapter 4

Careers

A sense of moral obligation pervades many of the conversations I have with graduate students as they prepare to enter the job market after graduation, with a number of them feeling torn between the need to make a living and the desire to do something personally meaningful with their lives. An abundance of jobs in architecture has made this choice even harder, since students can readily find employment and make a decent salary from the start. But students also know that most architectural firms serve the richest individuals and organizations, who control much of the wealth in the world, and that most people cannot afford to commission an architect, even if they wanted to. This creates an ethical dilemma for those who entered architecture with more altruistic aspirations.

Ethics can offer some useful ways of thinking about that dilemma. The twentieth-century philosopher John Rawls, in his seminal book *A Theory of Justice*, developed an argument that showed why we should care about the most disadvantaged among us (Rawls, 1971). He would have us imagine that, when deciding how to allocate resources, including the expertise of design professionals, we should act as if there is a "veil of ignorance" that prevents us from knowing our "original position" – whether or not we are the most or least advantaged person within a given population. If we did not know our status in terms of our own power or money, Rawls observed, we would allocate resources so that those who had the fewest resources would receive at least some benefit, since we might be that disadvantaged person. Equity, in other words, becomes not just something we should promote out of a sense of charity, but also out of self-interest.

Rawls's idea might strike some as a nice theory, but something that has little bearing on the real world, since most people do know their status in terms of money and power and their position in society in relation to others. Likewise, decision makers know full well who funds their campaigns or who has the most influence among their constituents, and so elected officials make resource allocations accordingly, often favoring those already favored by good fortune or at least an inherited one.

Figure 4.1 The dome of the main reading room at the Library of Congress in
Washington D.C. depicts human understanding partly lifting the veil of
ignorance, suggesting that no amount of knowledge will ever completely lift
the illusions that delude us.

But I have come to see the wisdom of Rawls's theory as I have watched
the fortunes of people take unexpected turns, sometimes for the worse. I
have seen my students lose parents and suddenly not have the money to
complete their education, my relatives lose a job and eventually have to
declare bankruptcy, or my colleagues not get tenure and quickly move on
to less lucrative and less secure adjunct teaching positions at various institutions. In other words, we all live with a "veil of ignorance" about what will
happen to us in the future: what setback, misfortune, or unexpected turn of
events will befall us. And those who think they are set for life may get the
greatest surprise when they discover that they are anything but set, and that
none of us really are.

For students contemplating their future careers, Rawls's idea can offer
some consolation. Because we cannot know the future, they should pursue
what they are most passionate about, since they will not know whether or
not it can become their career unless they try. Likewise, they should not take
a job just because it seems secure, since there is no guarantee that it will last
or that it will ensure a lifetime of financial security. Nor should the shy away
from helping the most disadvantaged people among us, since we may one day
be them for no fault of our own. This line of thought may sound depressing,

but my students don't find it so; it seems to help them see how many people live behind their own a veil of ignorance about themselves, thinking that they deserve the advantages that they have, which they often don't.

For many of my students, of course, what matters most to them is the pursuit of a professional career in architecture and if that means having to design for the wealthy clients who can afford their fees, then so be it. Rawls's argument offers a defense of that too. He did not say that people with resources should not have them; only that those who have resources have a self-interest in ensuring that those who don't have at least enough to lead a reasonable life. At the same time, I urge my students to look at the work that the world needs doing. This may sound baffling to some, since we rarely think about what the world wants, nor does "the world" have a list of what it needs done. But some students seem to see this as helpful advice because it leads them to consider not what they want, but what others need that they can help resolve. Better housing, safer streets, a cleaner environment: whatever the need, a way exists to achieve it and the jobs will eventually come to support it. That may not be the most lucrative work, perhaps, but it can be more satisfying work, helping others in ways that we would want others to help us.

Figure 4.2 The many favelas around the world show how much architects have yet to do. With billions of people living in such situations, there exists lifetimes of work to be done to alleviate such conditions.

Here, another line of ethical thought can come in handy. Kant believed that we should do what is right regardless of the consequences, and that we know what is right, regardless of what the skeptics might say. Architects know that creating a better environment for all people, regardless of their ability to pay design fees, remains at the core of the profession's responsibility, and all practitioners do that to some extent in every project. The benefits of buildings fall not just to the people who own or occupy them, but to all of the people employed to make or repair it, all the people who visit or walk by it, and all the people who may someday use or inhabit it long after we are gone. Architects have an obligation to design with all of them in mind.

Such a duty seems hard to meet since we cannot know all of the effects of our choices. We will never know all the people who have benefited – or not – from design decisions or all of the ways that what we do will get used in some far-off future. But that is just another form of Rawls's veil of ignorance. Not knowing the full consequences of what we do, we have to imagine the impact of our decisions on the most disadvantaged person conceivably affected by them and act in ways that would advantage them in some way. Here, the ability of the design mind to imagine what doesn't yet exist becomes especially useful. Architects always work behind a kind of veil of ignorance, never entirely sure what design decisions will lead to, and so acting in ways that minimize negative effects and maximize positive ones becomes central to the design process. Which makes it a fundamentally ethical one, in the sense that Rawls had in mind.

The architectural profession – like all professions – has a categorical imperative, to borrow Kant's phrase, to do the right thing and to practice in ways that benefit people far beyond those who we directly serve. We have to do so behind a veil of ignorance, unsure of the full effects of what we do and of who receives the most and the least advantages from what we decide, and so Rawls's thought experiment provides a useful measure stick, especially for students weighing their alternatives upon graduation. Professionals who do not at least try to improve the plight of the most disadvantaged among us may someday find themselves among the most disadvantaged of all.

Reference

Rawls, John. 1971. *A Theory of Justice*. Cambridge: Belknap Press of Harvard University Press.

Chapter 5

Codes

The Russian writer and critic, Victor Shklovsky once said that "Art makes the familiar strange so that it can be freshly perceived" (Shklovsky, 2004). Ethics does the same, not through visual means, but through words and questions, questions such as: Why do we organize the familiar world as we do, into public and private property, streets and sidewalks, buildings and landscapes? The world did not come to us this way – nature makes no such distinctions – and so why do we? For those who want to get on in the world and accept it the way it is, odd as that may be, such questions may seem irrelevant and maybe even annoying, but as Shklovsky rightly says, they are necessary if we hope to innovate. All creative activity, in other words, involves a degree of what Shklovsky called *estrangement*, or strange-making.

This can create conflicts, though, with efforts to codify the world. Communities write and enforce building and zoning codes to ensure that what gets built meets the expectations of the people who live there, however prejudicial that might be. Likewise, professions write and enforce codes of ethics to ensure that practitioners act in ways that serve the needs and interests of others and not just themselves. Such efforts have real benefit, but they run up against the creative urge to question them and to see how strange such codes really are. Promulgated for the sake of protecting public health, safety, and welfare, codes also represent the efforts of a relatively few experts to impose their ideas of what that entails on everyone else, few of whom have any say in what these codes contain or even in whether or not we need codes, at least as we think of them today.

What we codify – or not – also seems strange. Why do architects have so many local and national codes to follow, which ethicists as a field have relatively few beyond those of the laws of the land in which they live? Does that mean that we trust ethicists more than architects or just that architects' failure to preform has a potentially more-deadly effect on our lives than that of philosophers? Architects may gripe about codes, but practitioners know full well that such constraints also set limits that help define the nature and scope of their freedom to create. As Nietzsche once wrote, great artists "dance in chains," making their work look effortless despite – and

Figure 5.1 There is a spatial quality to ethics that rarely gets mentioned, but most cultures think of ethical behavior as moving upward and aiming higher, as this image suggests, and unethical actions as propelling us downward.

because of – the restraints placed on it by the community and by the artists themselves (Nietzsche, 1915, p. 140). Creativity involves not only seeing the strangeness of the world, but also pursuing the restrictions within which a good solution can emerge.

This suggests that we should seek out codes or create them if they don't. That certainly seems to be the case when it comes to codes of ethics: the fact that almost every profession has them should tell us something about their being an integral part and maybe even a defining characteristic of professionalism. Different professions, though, take diverse approaches to such codes. Some fields have very discipline-specific codes that pertain to what their practitioners do; the Hippocratic oath of doing no harm, for example, is clearly tied to medicine and rarely appears in the ethical codes of non-medical fields. In architecture, though, codes of ethics roam more widely, including provisions against activities such as giving or taking bribes, already against the law, that have no specific relationship to what architects do.

While that, too, seems strange, it may reflect the peculiar place that architecture plays in our lives. Buildings not only shelter us from the elements and provide us with the spaces in which we live and work; the construction industry also serves as ballast or a stimulus to nations' economies through governments' manipulation of interest rates and their subsidizing of home ownership and incentivizing of certain types of development. All of this involves a lot of money and a fair amount of risk to people if things don't go as planned, which puts architecture in the path of those who might want to game the system in their favor and which may explain why some obviously illegal activity has made it into some architectural codes of ethics.

Codes by their nature also define a set of minimum expectations, which can have the paradoxical or strange effect of lowering the bar when it comes to meeting those expectations. In building and zoning codes, such minimums ensure the protection of health, safety, and welfare, and we look to such codes not to produce great architecture, but to protect us from bad buildings.

Figure 5.2 The Majesty Building in Florida stood for over a decade unfinished, a reminder of the risk that accompanies the construction of buildings and a reflection of how much architecture and money – or the lack of it – can affect each other.

Lowering the bar on codes of ethics seems more curious. We don't want a practitioner to be just barely honest or minimally truthful; unlike the spectrum of good and bad buildings that we encounter in our lives, we seem to see ethics in more black-and-white terms. When we expect honesty and truthfulness from a professional, we want that in everything they do and say and not just in a minimal amount or only when required by a code. That may stem from the fact that building and zoning codes remain political documents, reflecting the values of what communities and the elected officials who represent them want in particular places in a specific time period, while codes of ethics seem to stand above that fray, embodying what we aspire to ourselves and hope to see in others.

That doesn't mean that codes of ethics don't change. They only change more slowly than zoning codes, as perhaps they should, since ethics evolves more slowly than the buildings. While human health, safety, and welfare all have moral dimensions and implications, ethics goes far beyond the minimum standards to urge us to be our very best in every situation, to do what is right regardless of the personal inconvenience, and to maximize our potential as human beings and as professionals. That such aspirations have been codified and that professionals largely adhere to them may be the strangest thing of all – and thankfully true.

References

Nietzsche, Friedrich. 1915. *Human, All Too Human: A Book for Free Spirits*. Bk 2. Chicago: Charles Kerr.

Shklovsky, Victor. 2004. "Art as Technique," in Julie Rivkin & Michael Ryan (eds.) *Literary Theory: An Anthology*. Malden, MA: Blackwell, 15–21.

Chapter 6

Collegiality

Ethical codes do not mean that everyone bound by them will always act ethically. I knew an architect, now deceased, who had designed the terminal at a small, regional airport several decades, but when it came time to add to the building, he lost the commission to a nationally known airport firm. He understood and accepted the official reason for the decision: the big firm offered the airport authorities the greatest assurance that they would get the best results for the limited public funds available. What bothered this local architect, though, was the new firm's rejection of his offer to give them his as-built drawings. They insisted that they needed to measure and redraw the original building for what the local architect thought were exorbitant fees, and he wondered if he should say anything to the client about it, or if that would look like bitterness for losing the commission and a lack of professionalism on his part.

When professionals vie for commissions, a thin line exists between competition and collegiality. Firms can compete among each other for one job and end up collaborating on the next, and so it becomes essential that they remain on good terms despite the disappointment when they lose a commission to their professional colleagues. This sharing of information and mutual support represents a generosity of spirit among professionals that rarely gets recognized in intensely capitalistic cultures, where we tend to reward fierce competitors, without giving nearly enough acknowledgment to the cooperation among rivals that makes healthy competition possible.

Specialization has made that cooperation both easier and harder than in the past. Architecture remained for a very long time what the critic Lewis Mumford called a "generalist profession," in which firms designed a wide variety of building types, but the specialization that Adam Smith saw as key to the success of capitalism has overtaken architecture as it has almost every other profession (Miller, 2002, p. 89). That has led many firms to focus on particular building types, often requiring that they travel ever further distances in pursuit of commissions in their area of specialization. Such firms typically find themselves competing more often for the same projects and so the rivalry among them can become fierce, even as their employees increasingly move

Figure 6.1 Airports have become environments that many people around the world share and their design reveals many of the tensions that exist in modern life, from security and safety of passengers to the joy and pain of people coming and going.

from one firm to another in the same area of expertise, leading to personal relationships across firm lines that inherently fosters cooperation.

Client interests have driven this rise of specialization. Clients who may not have commissioned many projects often want the benefit of a specialized firm's experience gained from other projects, which can minimize the risk that something might go wrong. At the same time, specialists presumably have the latest knowledge and information available to them, ensuring that the project represents a state-of-the-art effort. Finally, specialization can make a firm more efficient, reducing the time and presumably the cost required to do a project.

While local and less specialized firms may have the advantage of strong relationships with clients in their region, the lack of repeat work in any one building type makes it hard for these architects to specialize in anything, but that does not mean that they have no less cause to act generously to their more focused competitors. Firms working in far-off places, for example, frequently need a local representative on a project to help with approvals and construction observation. Generosity on the part of local practitioners to a nationally known competitor can lead to opportunities not otherwise available to them.

Generosity goes both ways, however. In the case of this airport commission, the specialized firm did not take the generous offer of the local architect to share the original drawings of the building. While that would have saved the client a lot of money, and the new firm a lot of time, it also apparently reduced the latter's ability to charge for additional services by doing their own measured drawings of the existing conditions. This may have come at the advice of their lawyers, who have become even more specialized and, in some ways, even more cautious as a result. Using someone else's drawings, even if the originals, could put the new firm in jeopardy if, for some reasons, those drawings had inaccuracies. A show of generosity on the part of one party can seem like a lot of liability or, at the same time, a lost opportunity on the part of another.

Accepting the generosity of others, though, is almost always the best course of action. Because the local architect remained friends with the officials who he had worked with on the airport, he did decide to let them know that the new firm had rejected his offer of the original drawings and were charging the client for making a new record of the building. The client decided to let the new firm proceed, but it did alert the airport authorities to the nature of the new firm and led to a heightened scrutiny of all of its work. A lack of generosity often breeds more of the same.

We can demonstrate generosity toward environments as much as toward other people. A university commissioned a local architect to design new energy-efficient lighting in a building that had won a number of design awards, using the standard fixture that the institution used in other campus structures. While the architect appreciated the client's interest in reducing energy costs, she questioned the use of a fixture that would conflict with the award-winning design and offered to investigate alternatives that would be more visually appropriate and just as energy efficient, but was told no by the client, who wanted to minimize maintenance costs.

How do we resolve conflicting but equally valid goals like these? The ethicist, Richard Rorty, argued that ethics has evolved to a point where absolute standards and singular criteria about what is right or wrong no longer serve us very well, and that it now consists of conversation among all who have a stake in the result, with the goal of finding a consensus based on weighing the consequences of different actions for different individuals or groups (Rorty, 1989). This architect took that tack. She had as many conversations as possible with as many different people as possible in order not only to understand the full extent of the issues involves, but also to listen for possible solutions in the comments of others. Design becomes, in that sense, a continual conversation about the right or wrong in a particular situation, a discussion that professionals should lead and may need to adjudicate, but

Figure 6.2 Great architects, like Steven Holl, integrate natural and artificial light in ways that makes any alterations to it akin to altering the art on display in his buildings, such as Kiasma, the Museum of Contemporary Art, shown here.

always remain open to, wherever the dialogue goes. In this case, the architect discovered a strong demand for the new lighting as well as some desire to respect certain features of the existing space, which she then did her best to address. Both of these examples suggest that ethics and design can help us resolve conflicts by being as collegial – and as conversational – as we can.

References

Miller, Donald. 2002. *Lewis Mumford: A Life*. New York: Grove Press.
Rorty, Richard. 1989. *Contingency, Irony and Solidarity*. New York: Cambridge University Press.

Chapter 7

Communication

I have spent a good part of my career writing about the built environment and editing the writing of others about it. While many of my architecture colleagues assumed that I had changed fields – that writing represented something fundamentally different from designing – I never saw it that way. Writing, for me, has always seemed like design in a different medium, using the same empathetic way of seeing a situation, in my case, the topic I am writing about and the audience I am writing to: the same formation of concepts, which in writing become concise statements rather than precise diagrams; and the same construction process, using words and grammar as opposed to building materials and physical structures.

The connections between writing and architecture go beyond such similarities in their methods to several parallels in their forms. For example, we typically enter a piece of writing as we do a building: directly, with a position statement that like an open door invites us into what lies beyond, or indirectly, with a process of discovery that draws us into a place with a degree of mystery or surprise. Likewise, we find our way through a written piece like a building. A single idea or narrative can work much like a main hallway directing us along, or a central event or turning point in the text can serve like the gathering point in a building to which every other space refers, or a series of unexpected plot twists or descriptions can lead us through sequentially, as in a building in which we don't exactly know where it ends.

In this sense, I've long adhered to Noam Chomsky's notion of a linguistic deep structure, not just because of the parallels that linguists have found among diverse languages but also because it seems to me that the spaces and sequences we create in the textual and the architectural worlds have so much in common (Chomsky, 2007). We organize our ideas in writing as we do our bodies in space and the clearer our understanding of those similarities, the better communicators we will be, whether using writing or designing as our means of doing so.

Because of that, I have also long felt frustration at the obfuscation that plagues architectural writing. I disliked as an editor of an academic journal often having to rewrite the prose of both architects and architectural faculty,

Figure 7.1 Rarely do we think of walking through a piece of writing as we do through a building or landscape, but the city of St. Paul, Minnesota, has employed poets to write poems that then get implanted into new sidewalks as part of its public works.

eventually giving up my role as one of the journal's editors; life is simply too short for such torturous work. But I still keep coming back to the belief that if architects and academics in the field understood writing as a form of design, they might one day do the former as well as they do the latter.

I remember once having to edit a piece by a well-known architectural critic who wrote an article so full of jargon words that I knew only a few fellow theorists would ever understand it. When I tried to translate the piece into prose that most readers would comprehend, the author demanded that I reinstate his original text since, as he admitted, he wanted to signal that he has read the current theoretical books and articles about the subject and that he was an insider, able to use the jargon associated with it.

This created an ethical dilemma for me. I knew that every discipline has its own jargon: words that have specialized meaning that only those in a field understand. And I know that such jargon has a purpose. It can enhance people's productivity by increasing the efficiency of conversation among those who understand it and encapsulate in a single word or phrase a complex theory or body of knowledge. In that sense, jargon increases communication by saving us time.

But jargon also diminishes communication by decreasing the ability of others outside a field to understand the lingo of those on the inside. To use an architectural analogy, jargon functions much like a gated community, inaccessible to most people. I recall using that analogy with this writer, making the claim that while his jargon-filled piece sounded progressive, it represented a very conservative position in that it excluded all but a very few. He was not amused.

He responded with the reasonable point that every field has its jargon and that the architectural profession is no different. I saw that as an unconvincing tit-for-tat argument: if writers in other fields write poorly and speak incomprehensibly, why can't we? He went on to say that readers should take some comfort in the jargon of others. If we have an illness or an injury needing immediate attention, we welcome the argot of medical personnel as they attend to us, speeding up the delivery of the treatment we need, even though we may also worry about what their conversation portends in terms of our prognosis. In situations like this, he said, we can find ourselves torn between a desire to understand a specialized terminology and a desire not to know.

Figure 7.2 While jargon can be an efficient way to communicate among technical professionals, it also has the effect of keeping other people away and, in cases like this train-related jargon, can have the opposite effect intended, leading to mistakes.

I laid out my ethical dilemma for him. As the editor, I could simply kill his piece if he chose to ignore my edits or I could publish the piece as he originally wrote it and let the readers decide what to make of it. Did I have a responsibility to my readers as the provider of readable prose or as a provocateur, presenting them with material they might not like or understand, but that they might at least like to know that it existed. Should I be a guard at the gated community of good communication or the anarchist who throws open the gates and invites everyone in?

If architecture, as Nietzsche wrote, is "an oratory to power by means of form," then might jargon an oratory to power by means of words? (2007, p. 69). Power relations, be they architectural or linguistic, bring us immediately to the question of who has power over whom, by what means, and to what end? If the power that professionals wield has, as its goal, improving the lives of others – as in the case of attending physicians or, one hopes, in the case of architects looking after the public's health, safety, and welfare – then we happily grant them that power through their license to practice. But it quickly becomes an abuse of power if professionals simply want to show, through their actions or their words, that they know or possess something others do not.

Or was my editorial gatekeeping itself the exertion of my own will-to-power over that of the writer? I ended up resisting the temptation to reduce every conflict to a question of power and decided that I had an obligation, contra Nietzsche, to defend the interests of those with less power – the readers in this case – against a writer who wanted to use jargon to assert his power over them and to elevate himself in the eyes of a few peers. I killed the piece – and the writer has not spoken to me since.

References

Chomsky, Noam. 2007. *On Language*. New York: The New Press.
Nietzsche, Friedrich. 2007. *Twilight of the Idols*. Hertfordshire, England: Wordsworth.

Chapter 8

Competition

I have never been a particularly competitive person, since competition tends to frame the world in a false binary of winners and losers. Indeed, I think competition has a deeply paradoxical quality, in which those who view themselves as winners ultimately lose and those viewed as losers ultimately win: "Blessed are the meek, for they shall inherit the earth," as Jesus so succinctly put it (Matthew 5:5). Still, competition continues to rule, at least in market economies, and those of us who prefer collaboration over competition and win/win solutions over win/lose ones have only to wait for the paradoxes to begin.

For architects, competition presents a particular kind of paradox. The very nature of design, as a process, involves the resolution of conflicting goals and competing agendas among the people served by it. Architecture resists antagonism. A building that did not achieve as many win/win solutions as possible would not function very well nor last long, since those in it who felt they had lost too much in its design would not care to stay very long in it or care very much for it. At the same time, architects must compete for work and win commissions that their colleagues lose, a condition that runs counter to what those architects must do the moment they win the competition, which is to collaborate.

Another paradox here lies in the fact that, while design arises out of collaboration and cooperation, the architectural culture participates in a lot of competitions. If we do not do well with competition, why do we hold competitions? The first code of ethics promulgated by the American Institute of Architects in 1909 discouraged its members from taking part in unpaid competitions. "It is unprofessional for an architect . . . to take part in any competition the terms of which are not in harmony with the principles approved by the Institute" which included the condemnation of "The offering of professional services . . . without compensation." (AIA, 1909) Architects back then understood that participating in uncompensated competitions amounted to a form of self-exploitation, but that did not last in the face of anti-trust worries later in the century, when regulators might see forbidding such competitions as anti-competitive.

Figure 8.1 The Sydney Opera House, designed by Jørn Utzon, was one of the most famous competition winners, where a jury of architects, including architect Eero Saarinen, selected a building that became an icon for an entire nation.

That code of ethics also stipulated against other unfair competitive practices. An example of that: an architectural firm, seeking a commission at a university, contacted a major donor of the school that the partners in the firm knew, to use the donor's leverage in the institution to get the firm hired, even though the building committee and the dean wanted to hire another architect for the job. The dean acquiesced to the donor's wishes but was furious at the firm for applying pressure like that.

In the competitive marketplace for services, enterprises often use whatever advantage they have to convince a customer or client to choose them over others. That often takes the form of persuasion, convincing the client in an interview, for example, that one's firm will do the best job. But in cases like this, in which the partners know a donor who has some leverage with the client, the competitive advantage takes the form of outside pressure, a quid-pro-quo in which the favor of donating money gets returned as a favor of hiring the donor's architects.

In most cases, complying with a donor's wishes turns out fine; the architect does a good job and everyone ends up happy. But in the situation here, in which the dean and building committee had already decided to go with another firm, the pressure applied by the donor at the request of the architects made the latter an unwelcome interloper in the selection process. The dean and faculty, of course, did not have to acquiesce to the donor's wishes, but doing so would have harmed that relationship, which clearly the school did not want to do.

The dean also could have directed her annoyance at the donor for agreeing to apply the pressure in the first place. But, when the school's leadership heard that the donor had done it as a favor to the firm, the dean focused her anger on the architects, even though she agreed to commission them to do the project. There was nothing explicitly unethical in what the architects did. The commercial world works this way, sometimes pressuring clients when persuasion doesn't work. But while not unethical, the architects' actions put them in the unenviable position of starting a relationship with an angry and distrustful client. That raises the bar on what the architects have to achieve, proving that, despite the unfortunate start to the project, they will do the best job. And it also raises the bar for the client, in setting aside the initial anger to build a relationship of mutual trust with the architects and to remain open to what they have to offer.

This leads to what the philosopher H. J. N. Horsburgh has called "the ethics of trust" (Horsburgh, 1960), in which people seem more likely to trust people in general than specific individuals who have violated our trust before. The dean has to trust the donor's judgment in accepting his recommendation of the architectural firm, the donor has to trust the architects in their doing a good job so as not to harm the school he has contributed

Figure 8.2 Architects' use of personal connections to receive commissions has a long history. Wallace Harrison, whose architectural firm designed Empire Plaza in Albany, New York, had a family connection, through marriage, to the governor, Nelson Rockefeller.

to, and the architects have to earn the trust of the dean in going forward. Earning and keeping the trust of others requires that we act with the utmost ethical as well as professional care, being absolutely virtuous (fair, prudent, and honest, for example), attending to all aspects of our duty (to the client, school, and community), and weighing the consequences of everything we do (in terms of the budget, schedule, and the greatest good of the students and staff). Ethics, in other words, offers a roadmap for winning and keeping others' trust in competitive situations. And if it cannot meet that bar, this firm would be better off declining the commission, for the distrust of the client would only grow.

References

American Institute of Architects. 1909. *The American Architect*, 1774, December, 272–274

Horsburgh, H. J. N. 1960. "The Ethics of Trust," *Philosophical Quarterly*, 10, October, 343–54.

Matthew, 5:5, The Bible. 1952. TLB. New York: Thomas Nelson & Sons.

Chapter 9

Conflicts of commitment

Declining commissions may not seem wise, but in some situations it can be the wisest possible path. An architect in my community serves on a state board that selects firms for public projects, and her husband is an architect whose office benefits from the board's decisions. While the architect on the board excuses herself from deliberations that involve her husband's firm, many practitioners think that her knowledge of the board and her collegiality with board members gives her husband's firm an unfair advantage. Such conflicts of commitment comprise the most frequent ethical issue in most workplaces and as anyone who has filled out a conflict-of-interest statement knows, this mainly involves revealing the conflict and mitigating it in some way. This architect did this: she acknowledged her conflict with her husband and recused herself from pertinent discussions.

But conflicts-of-commitment involve perception as much as execution and if others still think a conflict exists – or that the steps to mitigate it do not go far enough – then the ethical issue remains: at what point does a person have to step aside or quit doing something altogether in order to end the sense that others have of unfairness? Where should this architect's loyalties lie? The philosopher Josiah Royce argued that loyalty represents the greatest virtue because it embodies our adherence to something larger than ourselves, to an ideal or even a noble or "lost cause" (Royce, 1988, p. 324). Royce recognized that evil also seeks our loyalty and he made a distinction between the "true loyalty" of people who seek the good of others, and "predatory loyalty" that destroys the ability of other individuals or communities to remain loyal to their own ideals.

A paradox, in other words, lies at the very heart of the concept of loyalty: it is a good thing, unless it negates the loyalties of others, in which it becomes a bad thing. The context and consequences of loyalty thus become paramount in determining its value. We literally cannot say whether or not a person's loyalty to something is good or bad without seeing what it stems from and where it leads to, and in that sense, blind loyalty to something regardless of its intentions or its effects is no loyalty at all. For this architect, or anyone for that matter who has divided loyalties, Royce's ideas can

Figure 9.1 The Forbidden City in Beijing shows how governments have used architecture to enforce the loyalty of their people, some of which may be the loyalty of true believers and some of which may be the predatory kind.

help sort out what to do. Royce makes the distinction between loyalty to an ideal supported by what he called "genuine communities," and loyalty to groups that have vicious or destructive intentions akin to the survival of the fittest in nature, which he called "natural communities" (Royce, 1988, pp. 224–225).

When we find ourselves with divided loyalties to different groups, Royce's argument suggests that we need to look carefully at the intentions, methods, and consequences of each community to which we hold allegiance. This architect has one loyalty to her husband, another to the board on which she serves, another still to the people of the state and to the profession to which she belongs. How should she choose among them or prioritize one over the others? Royce makes a distinction that can help her decide. He argued that communities come before individuals and that the very idea of an individual is incoherent unless viewed within the context of a group. Language, for example, only has value if others understand it; a "private language," as Ludwig Wittgenstein argued, literally makes no sense (1958, p. 98). The same applies to other human activities as well: those that benefit only individuals at the expense of communities do not deserve our loyalty.

Putting the community coming before the individual is something that not only this architect should consider, but that the profession she belongs to often represents. While architects may serve individual clients, their role as a profession – like any profession – has to put the community first, prioritizing the public good over private goods. In architecture, for example, that can take the form of zoning regulations, building codes, and planning committees, charged with ensuring that private development also generates public benefit or at least does not detract from the common good and the health, safety, and welfare of its occupants. While architects will sometimes complain about such constraints, the loyalty of the profession to them remains strong, evident in the numbers of architects who sit on such boards or contribute to the writing of such regulations.

Architects also show that loyalty through a firm's design work. However much a building serves the needs of its clients and occupants, and meets the health, safety, and welfare requirements of the codes, what deserves the name architecture also improves the public realm, attends to the community interest, and seeks out a greater good. That can take the form of providing amenities accessible to the larger public, respecting the views and solar access of neighboring structure, minimizing the use of energy in its operations, and using low-impact or recyclable materials, among many other methods.

Figure 9.2 Buildings contribute a lot of carbon to the atmosphere and strategies such as the thermal rock wall that Jeremy Levine developed for a house in California show how the design professions can innovate, with walls that absorb heat during the day and radiate indoors at night.

When people talk about the power of architecture, they frequently refer to its physical characteristics – its space, form, and materials – but its power also lies in its ethical qualities: its ability to provide benefits for people far beyond its immediate users, be they passersby, future occupants, other species, or the public in general. Therein lies the true loyalty of the profession, as Royce would say: loyalty to the ideal or noble cause of having responsibilities that transcend our immediate circle of family, friends, and colleagues, and that involve those who will never meet.

The problem faced by this architect on the state board looms larger than just a personal conflict of interest; it represents a professional conflict as well. Practitioners have a monopoly in the marketplace by virtue of their licensure and so already have a position of power that, if perceived by the public as being used for personal benefit, can tarnish more than just the individual architects involved. At the same time, if the architecture that comes from the decisions of that state board seems tainted by a board member caring more for her husband's firm than for the public good, the very idea of architecture as a public benefit gets tarnished as well.

Royce's idea of loyalty makes this architect's choice `clear. She needs to step down from the board or her husband's firm needs to agree not to pursue state work while she sits on the board. While the others in his firm may not like that prohibition, it may be their wisest course, since even the appearance of a conflict of interest may lead other board members to hesitate awarding the firm a state project, even if well qualified for it. Royce once wrote that "the world is a progressively realized community of interpretation," and those who do not realize – and respect – that community of interpretation will pay dearly as a result (1988, p. 317).

References

Royce, Josiah. 1988. *Josiah Royce: Selected Writings*. John Edwin Smith and William Kluback (eds.). Mahwah, NJ: Paulist Press.
Wittgenstein, Ludwig. 1958. *Philosophical Investigations*. Oxford: Blackwell

Chapter 10

Creativity

The human brain seems hard-wired for creativity. Neuroscientists once thought that the brain worked like a large machine, a mainframe computer able to process a lot of information, but research in that field has shown that our brains work more like a large room full of personal computers, networked together, with each storing a different kind of data. We now know that when each of us encounters an object for the first time, for example, the word for it goes in one part of the brain, its function in another, its appearance in yet another and so on (Koutstaal, 2012). That sorting of data about the world in different parts of the brain is more efficient, allowing us to store much more information that we could if every object and experience we encountered had its own unique neural connection. That sorting also makes the brain more effective by identifying similar objects to what we have experienced before, allowing us to identify it by bringing together the distributed data in our brains and to see enough similarity – or difference – to judge the degree to which the new one compares to the old.

That cognitive distribution of data allows the human brain to be more creative as well. Creative people do not just come upon new ideas out of the blue; instead, creative work involves a rigorous, systematic, and self-critical process of intentionally recombining the data we have experienced. Like solving a complicated math equation, creative problem-solving involves keeping a number of variables constant and altering one or a few at a time to see what that produces, learning from what does not work, and trying a new combination of variables until coming upon a solution that resolves as much of the problem as efficiently, elegantly, and effectively as possible. In that light, coming up with new ideas is something anyone can do, since those who have their full cognitive capacity are born with this capability, evident in the creative ways in which children play with little or no formal education or instruction. It is also something we can learn or rather re-learn. Born to be creative, people often get subjected to educational systems that seem determined to drum that creative impulse out of us, forcing us to have to re-learn, when older, what we knew as children: how to combine things in playful and unexpected ways to come up with something new and more interesting.

Figure 10.1 Children demonstrate, through their interactions with their built environment, that we are all born with the capacity to be creative and to imagine new forms of play and interpret settings in unexpected ways.

The reason for the educational system's general hostility to creativity has something to do with the way in which nineteenth- and twentieth-century economies worked. Employers needed people who could read, write, and calculate in order to run the machines on the factory floors or manage the operations in the office buildings, and with that in mind, primary and secondary education in the developed world evolved into one that graded students according to the correctness – rather than the creativity – of their school work. Children got good at taking assignments, doing their homework, and giving the information back to their teachers on tests to show the level of understanding. Rarely did this process accommodate the "wrong" answer to a problem that might turn out to be the creative new insight, in part because those charged with running large organizations did not necessarily want employees who challenged assumptions or raised uncomfortable questions.

The needs of the twenty-first-century economy have changed, however, and the educational system has not kept up. In a high-speed, global economy, innovation and creativity have become key ingredients in the success not just of organizations, but also individuals; with so much to choose from, consumers select what stands out from all the rest, what meets a need in a new way, and what solves a problem inexpensively and elegantly. This has led to a growing interest in design thinking or human-centered design in fields as diverse as public health, public policy, and business, among many others.

While most in the design disciplines continue to focus on designing physical products and environments – the goods side of the economy – the greatest growth in demand has occurred where few designers have yet to go: applying design methods to processes and systems – the services side of the economy.

Apart from the Financial Crash of 2008, which led to a lot of layoffs within the design community, the demand for new products and places has remained high as the result of a burgeoning economy and a rapidly growing population, and so architects and designers have had relatively little incentive to shift their focus to service design. Which is too bad, since we have all suffered from poorly conceived services and systems created by people and policy makers who did not know how to design, and which has led to all sorts of unintended consequences and undesirable impacts as a result. Recognizing this, organizations and communities have started to seek out designers able to think more creatively and holistically about services and systems, raising the question: how do designers come up with new ideas?

Not every situation, of course, requires redesign. For systems and services that still work well and simply need to be made more efficient, the business world has evolved several effective management techniques. Design proves most useful when a process or procedure requires complete rethinking, a paradigm shift of some sort or a whole new idea, and acknowledging the limits of the design process, as well as its value, constitutes a key ethical obligation of every professional. Knowing when to say no is just as important as getting to yes.

At the same time, the rise of service design has forced the design community to pay more attention to its epistemology, to how we know what we know. The traditional focus on the goods side of the economy has enabled designers to judge their work according to its physical outcomes and to put relatively little emphasis on the thinking that led to those results. Indeed, star designers and professors have tended to mystify the design process, as if solutions arise by magic rather than through the systematic and rigorous ways in which the creative mind actually works. While it varies in subtle ways from one creative person to another, the steps in this process follow a similar path:

1 Doing the background research and observation needed to understand a situation
2 Framing and re-framing the problem to see it in new ways
3 Generating ideas based on experiences and on analogies to other seemingly unrelated phenomena, and
4 Modeling and testing the results to see what meets the needs of the situation within the given or self-imposed constraints.

The design process has evolved over the history of our species since it has proven effective in generating new ideas and coming up with new strategies.

Figure 10.2 Design's greatest value may lie in how it helps us arrive at new solutions to old problems, helping us think outside the box, sometimes literally, as Frank Gehry did when he created more space inside the Vitra Design Museum by bringing the stair outside the wall.

Creativity involves seeing the world in unconventional ways and the initial observation phase of a project holds out the opportunity to not only record and understand a situation, but to comprehend it from the perspective of others, which remains fundamental not only to creativity, but also to ethics, as it helps us see an action or outcome from as many diverse points of view as possible.

That repositioning of one's perspective toward a situation leads to the next phase: re-framing the problem in order to open it up to alternative interpretations and new connections. Too often, designers and non-designers alike solve the wrong problem beautifully, which helps explain why so many of the most wicked problems never seem to get resolved: we tend to focus on problems we already know how to solve and ignore the complex ones with which we don't know what to do. New ideas can also arise through analogies with seemingly unrelated situations or solutions.

The radical collaboration that characterizes most design teams as they work across many sectors of the economy and with diverse disciplines provides an ideal way to incubate new ideas, which typically arises out of the combination, appropriation, or re-interpretation of existing ones. Finally, in the model-building and evaluation phase of work, new ideas emerge when facing a previous failure. The only real failure in creative work is failing to see the possibilities and to seize the opportunities of failure.

New ideas have the same source as every idea: in our brains and out of our experiences. Their newness stems from simply putting existing ideas together in new ways to see what happens, embracing failure as something from which to learn rather than to avoid. And getting others to buy into a new idea involves bringing them along in the same process, co-creating with them so that they, too, can remember how it felt to be the creative people they once were, like children playing on the playground of life.

Reference

Koutstaal, Wilma. 2012. *The Agile Mind*. New York: Oxford University Press.

Chapter 11

Data

The widely accepted idea that humans remain the most intelligent creatures on the planet has always seemed to me to be as self-serving as it is self-delusional. We define intelligence in a way that makes us seem intelligent and that definition rests on evidence that only we determine, which makes it a tautology. Who is to say that I am more intelligent than, say, the dog at my feet, nose to the air, able to smell things I never will, and unperturbed by the news of the day, accepting the world as it is with a stoicism that few humans will ever attain? While my dog doesn't have the human capability, as the historian Yuval Noah Harari argues in his book *Sapiens*, to act flexibly and in large numbers, which has led to humanity's dominance of the planet, my dog is more a part of the natural world than I am, a world that collectively has far more intelligence in the sense of having more information and complexity than humanity ever will (Harari, 2015).

Which should cause us to question Harari's claim in his book *Homo Deus* that humanity may one day be replaced by machines more intelligent than us (Harari, 2017). Harari argues that "organisms are algorithms and life is data processing" and that "non-conscious but highly intelligent algorithms may soon know us better than we know ourselves," ending with the question of "what will happen to society, politics, and daily life" when this happens? (pp. 396–397). While Harari rightfully challenges our "inflated human pride and prejudices" in seeing "ourselves as the apex of creation," he goes on to make the questionable statement that "whenever an animal ceased to fulfill any function at all, it went extinct," and that this may be humanity's fate once we no longer have a function after the "Internet-of-All-Things is up and running" (p. 395).

Harari commits a factual error here. The extinction of animals has almost nothing to do with whether they have a function: in ecosystems, all animals have a function and while our actions can threaten their existence, it does not depend upon their usefulness to us. Indeed, such a statement reflects the inflated human pride that Harari criticizes. Likewise, humanity will continue to have a function even if we end up creating technology smarter – and one hopes, wiser – than us. If anything, we may finally achieve what other

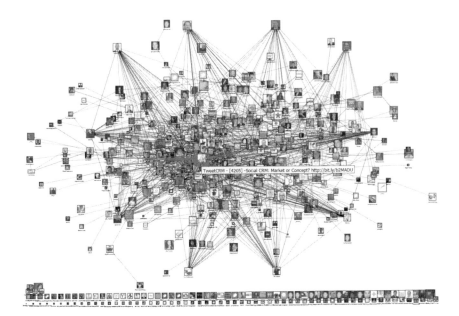

Figure 11.1 This image of Twitter users who mentioned "Social CRM" on April 6, 2010, scaled by number of followers, raises ethical questions about what constitutes private information and who has the right to access it.

animals have long had: a greater connection to and integration with the natural world, and a more benign role, ecologically, than we have had over the last 10,000 years.

Harari invents a term – Dataism – to define the "data religion" based on the belief that "the universe consists of data flows, and the value of any phenomenon or entity is determined by its contribution to data processing" (p. 367). He acknowledges that Dataism "inverts the traditional pyramid of learning" from data to information to knowledge to wisdom and that "humans can no longer cope with the immense flows of data," which should "therefore be entrusted to electronic algorithms, whose capacity far exceeds that of the human brain." He goes on to say that "Dataists are skeptical about human knowledge and wisdom, and prefer to put their trust in Big Data and computer algorithms" (p. 368).

Like all human beliefs, this argument does not rest on logic nor does it acknowledge its own flaws. As one of the first social scientists, Giambattista Vico argued persuasively in 1725, we can never know what we did not create, which suggests that no amount of Big Data will ever fully comprehend the natural world, which neither humans nor machines generated (Vico, 2000). While we and our machines should continue to gather data about the world, no amount of data will ever fully describe reality since, by definition, that reality is ever larger than all the data we can collect about it. And, ironically, one of the activities on the planet most vulnerable to extinction is Big Data itself, the collection of which requires amounts of energy, water, and rare minerals that may exceed our ability or the ability of machines to sustain.

Harari's argument echoes those of techno-futurist architects of the last century, who envisioned a future in which humans would have extensive leisure as our machines did all the work. That reductive argument ran aground because people do not want leisure, however much they may yearn for it in the abstract, and instead want to do meaningful work – to have a function, as Harari might say. Rather than imagining machines replacing humans because we would no longer have a function, we should ask what machines can do better than we can so that we can focus more on what we do better than machines.

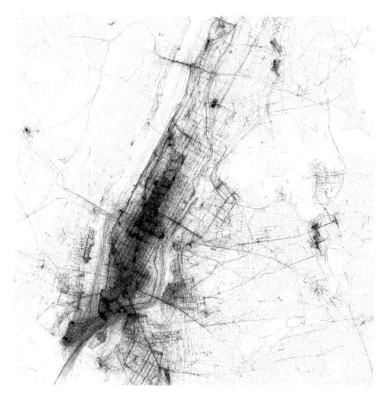

Figure 11.2 Data mapping allows us to understand human behavior in new and more visual ways. This map shows the distributed way locals take photos in New York City versus the highly concentrated photos of tourist. The ethics has to do with how this information gets used and by whom.

Harari's "data religion" raises other questions as well. Religions, as Harari notes in his history of the species, create fictions that people believe in and that thus become real to them, despite the fact that there exists no data to back it up. What does it mean, then, to have a religion of data, when data has nothing to do with religion? And what ethical questions does such a religion raise, such as: what data is being collected, about whom, for what end, and to whose benefit? While religions have prompted their share of bloodshed, as Christopher Hitchens argued in his book *God is Not Great: How Religion Poisons Everything* (Hitchens, 2007), religions have all tried to help people come to terms with our fallibility and mortality. To conceive of a religion – Dataism – that will lead to the extinction of humanity seems not only perverse, but ethically untenable and morally objectionable to say the least. While Hitchens does not do enough to recognize the good that religion has done in the world, his argument about the poison that comes with all true believers certainly applies to Harari's Dataists. Religious fanaticism requires our resistance. And in the face of Dataism, refusing to share personal information and disconnecting from the Internet-of-All-Things may be one of the most important ethical stances to take. Infidels in the religion of data, unite!

References

Harari, Yuval Noah. 2015. *Sapiens: A Brief History of Humankind*. New York: HarperCollins.

Harari, Yuval Noah. 2017. *Homo Deus: A Brief History of Tomorrow*. New York: HarperCollins.

Hitchens, Christopher. 2007. *God is Not Great: How Religion Poisons Everything*. New York: Hachette.

Vico, Giambattista. 2000. *New Science*. New York: Penguin.

Chapter 12

Deception

Over the course of 19 years as a dean, I saw how much expense universities incur when looking for faculty and academic leaders, especially because of the frequency with which these searches fail. While that sometimes happens when the institution cannot find the right person for the position, a surprising number of failed searches occur when candidates turn down attractive job offers, usually because they had no intention of taking the job in the first place. To outsiders, such insincere job applicants can seem selfish, as if they go through this process to stoke their egos rather than to seek new employment. And to critics of the cost of higher education, it certainly represents a waste of time and money on the part of both the institutions seeking people and the home institutions of these candidates, who frequently use their job offer to get higher pay or some other retention package in exchange for staying.

There is nothing illegal about turning down a job offer, but the number of times I have seen this happen makes me wonder about the ethics of such behavior. If, after going through interviews, candidates find out things about the position or institution that make them change their mind, that is fine. When they have no intention of taking the position, regardless of the offer, that represents a level of deception that can also backfire. For example, candidates take a risk that their home institutions will make a counter offer to get them to stay. I have seen some get called on their deception and not get a retention package, in which case they either have to take a new job they don't really want or to stay with their existing employer who didn't care to retain them and so doesn't really want them all that much either.

Deception on the part of faculty when looking for jobs also goes against the ethics of academic research. Research rests on an idea that dates back to the ancient Greeks: that ethical actions stem from the virtue of those engaged in the activity. While we may value research according to its consequences – did it result in new knowledge or a useful discovery? – we also depend upon researchers' integrity, honesty, and fairness in order to trust their conclusions. The research community has put in place mechanisms to ensure such trustworthiness. The anonymous or "blind" review of a scientific paper by

Figure 12.1 Research, such as that which occurs at the Salk Institute, rests upon the ethics of honesty, fairness, prudence, and even courage in the face of public opposition. The research community enforces such ethics to ensure the best work.

peers prior to its publication and the replication of a scientific experiment by others to see if the same outcomes occur represent two effective ways of catching unreliable or unverifiable results.

The so-called theological virtues of faith, hope, charity, and love also have relevance to research. Although we often think of science and faith as sharply divided, researchers have to have a degree of faith in the value of their work and hope in its ultimate success. At the same time, they have to love what they do, given the long hours devoted to their pursuits, and to have a charitable respect for the work of others. In research, as in all creative activity, we cannot entirely disconnect good work from the goodness of the people doing it.

Some in the architectural community have discounted the relevance of this to their careers. I have heard colleagues rightly argue that architects have a long history of deploying deception in buildings to achieve aesthetic or practical ends: using blank windows to make the front of a building symmetrical, encased columns to make their support appear more substantial, and tapered roofs to make their edge appear thinner. Deceptions like these

Figure 12.2 Useful deception has long played a part in architecture, as in Christopher Wren's attic level at St. Paul's Cathedral in London, which looks like another floor level, but which really screens a sloped roof behind it.

appeal to people's sense of architectural correctness and visual rightness and as such, they seem more receptive than deceptive. But when a deception happens in order to advantage some people over others, it has no such appeal.

I have heard other architectural colleagues argue a more philosophical point on the matter. For some of them, architecture entails the speculation upon future possibilities rather than the discovery of facts about the world as it exists, which suggests that the "truth" of a speculation rests upon its ability to convince people of its value, not upon its verifiability. Meanwhile others have questioned the objectivity of all human activity, science included. This more radical idea doesn't distinguish between design and science, but instead sees a degree of subjectivity and cultural relativity in both.

Such arguments, however, do not diminish the role of virtue: in even the most subjective or speculative work, integrity, honesty, and fairness matter. Nor do the virtues essential to research end there. The cardinal virtues of prudence, temperance, fortitude, and justice also apply: research demands the use of good judgment or prudence, a temperate sense of balance and reasonable limits, the fortitude to keep pursuing a promising idea despite setbacks or unexpected results, and a just concern that the results have widespread benefits. Without such ethics, the academy would not function.

Nor would professional practice. When adjunct faculty use a design studio to get students' ideas for projects in the office, when a developer client pressures architects to share their ideas about a project with no intention of giving them the commission, or when institutions stage a competition to get design ideas with little or no compensation for all of the architects involved, we see different levels of deception at work. The response, so often heard, that no one forced anyone to take part in these activities is true, but it seems equally true that free markets have power differences that give some a great deal of leverage over others. Free markets give way more freedom to some rather than others.

Ethicists has argued that deception or a lack of honesty in dealing with others doesn't pay, but that often doesn't seem true. Deception clearly pays for at some – the deceptive candidate, the conniving client, the predatory professor – at least for the short term. The price gets paid over the long term when word gets out about deceptive behavior that leads to others distrusting the perpetrator. Eventually, the job offers end, the competitions fail, and the students vote with their feet. A reputation for dishonesty becomes almost impossible to shake and those who deny that are just deceiving themselves.

Chapter 13

Disasters

In my first year in architecture school, I drove with a professor and a group of fellow students to Elmira, New York, to help homeowners dig out the mud that had filled their houses after a catastrophic flood. I remember standing knee-deep in mucky basements, filling buckets and emptying them into dumpsters, returning to campus at the end of the day exhausted and coated in drying dirt. After the intensely intellectual work of first year design studio, I felt good engaging with homeowners and buildings in such a physical, visceral way and wondered why this, too, wasn't a normal part of architectural education. If we design and oversee the construction of buildings, shouldn't we also attend to them when disaster strikes, in the same way that doctors attend to people's health in the wake of an epidemic or earthquake?

This seems particularly pertinent in this century. While we have already had our share of social, technological, and economic disruptions, the disasters that have killed the most people or upended the most lives have had mainly natural causes: from the 2003 heatwave in Europe that killed 35,000 people in one month, to the devastation of the entire island of Puerto Rico by Hurricane Maria in 2017. Because of the increasing intensity of meteorological events around the world, some experts estimate that many millions of people may become environmental refugees over the course of this century, fleeing coastal flooding and inland droughts, with hundreds of thousands of people dying annually from contaminated water and poor sanitation connected to these disruptions (Azhar, 2017).

The need for better-designed systems, structures, and settlements has become a top priority, and not just for those fleeing unhealthy environments. Poor sanitation and overcrowding provides breeding grounds for disease that affect everyone. The devastating 2010 earthquake in Haiti offers a case in point. Although extreme in terms of the number of lives lost, that quake remains one of many disasters that have been occurring with ever-greater frequency around the globe. The United Nations has tracked natural catastrophes back to 1900, with some startling findings. Since the 1950s, for example, the number of weather-related disasters such as droughts and floods has increased over nine-fold, geological disasters

Figure 13.1 The flooding that has followed hurricanes can create some of the greatest damage to buildings and neighborhoods, and these events, once rare, have become increasingly common in the wake of storms that are increasingly violent.

such as earthquakes have quadrupled, and biological disasters such as epidemics have, amazingly, multiplied by a factor of 200. North America has had more than its share of these events. In 2005, the last date of these statistics, the United States ranked third among countries most often hit by natural disasters (Haiti was ninth) and it led the world in the cost of these events (Canada was 22nd). The US and Canada together absorbed over $372 billion (US) dollars in disaster-related damages between 1991 and 2005 (NOAA, 2018).

Disasters, in other words, have become both more common and costly and we will likely see more situations like the one in Haiti in the years ahead. While we can't always predict *when* natural disasters will occur, we can predict *where* they will likely happen and *what* effect they will have. With urban slums, according to the UN (2018), growing at the rate of 78 million people a year, and with many slum dwellers living in inadequate shelter on marginal land, often in seismically active and drought- or flood-prone regions, we can predict where the largest disasters, in terms of loss of life, will next likely take place. And we have to look to our own shores to see where the costliest calamities will occur. Hurricane Katrina remains the single most expensive catastrophe since 1900, says the UN, and, with much of the densely populated North American coastline so hazard-prone, we can imagine where even more costly disasters may someday happen.

The design professions have long benefited from disasters. A great deal of architectural work, for example, happened in the wake of the 1871 Chicago fire and the 1906 San Francisco earthquake, although the architectural discipline has not always responded in the most enlightened way to these catastrophes. As Gladys Hansen and Emmet Condon argue in their book *Denial of Disaster*, the rebuilding of post-earthquake San Francisco followed looser building codes than those in place before the quake in order to speed reconstruction (Hanson & Condon, 1989). In that sense, architects have sometimes been overly eager and perhaps unwitting participants in what Naomi Klein, in her book *The Shock Doctrine*, calls the "disaster-capitalism complex, in which all conflict- and disaster-related functions. . . [including] rebuilding cities. . . can be performed by corporations at a profit" (Klein, 2007, p. 12).

Acknowledging this past becomes particularly relevant as we face situations like that of Haiti, and a sizable number of designers have done work relevant to the needs of people after natural disasters. At my university, a colleague, John Dwyer, and a his students developed a "Clean Hub," which can provide clean water, composting toilets and solar power generation, all

Figure 13.2 Shigeru Ban's paper-tube structural systems provide shelter for people displaced by disasters and forced to construct houses themselves. Ban's designs allow for quick deployment by low-skilled labor.

packed into a shipping container or panel truck and deliverable to disaster sites. And other groups, such as Rotary International, have developed emergency response kits that meet the basic needs of families after a disaster until more permanent shelter comes. Still, given the magnitude of the problem globally and the number of lives and amount of money potentially saved by a more pro-active approach to disasters, the attention the design professions have paid to the problem so far pales in comparison to its importance.

This stems in part, from the dominant approach to design practice. Designers mostly work with individual clients, as doctors do with individual patients, to develop custom solutions to site-specific problems. Such practices serve well the relatively small part of the human population that can afford such custom attention, but remains inadequate to the needs of people globally, whose long-term needs involve sanitation, clean water, and safe and secure shelter. Public health offers an alternative practice, focusing not on individual needs, but on finding appropriate, prototypical solutions that are simple and cost effective enough for widespread implementation over the long term by large numbers of people.

Examples of that public-health approach sometimes occur in architecture schools, when a studio addresses low-cost housing, for instance, or when a class looks at appropriate technology or takes on a community project for people in need. But the dominance of the medical model of practice in the architecture schools and the architectural profession greatly limits the number of people we can serve, making it hard for us to intervene effectively in disasters like that of Haiti, where nowhere near enough time or money exists for a client-based approach to design.

Public-health professionals also do more than respond to disasters. In contrast to medicine, which, like design, tends to react to the problems that others present, public health puts much more emphasis on prevention, on changing the conditions that lead to problems in the first place. A public health version of design could do the same, identifying those places most in need of immediate attention, where intervention now would prevent the greatest expense and largest loss of life in the future. Disaster-prone areas offer the best place to start. A prevention-oriented model of design practice would involve a more entrepreneurial way of operating, in which architects would not wait for commissions to come to them but would instead pro-actively approaches communities or even entire countries with appropriate and affordable ideas of how to avoid the next likely disaster. Design fees would become less a cost and more a form of insurance, a current investment to protect against future losses.

In the face of a waning demand for traditional design services and the growing frequency of natural disasters directly affecting the built environment and its inhabitants, a prevention-oriented, public-health version of the design fields may soon become the fastest growing areas of design practice. And with that growth will come a change in professional ethics.

Architectural ethics has traditionally focused on our duties to the general public and to clients, with little mention to our responsibilities to the poorest and neediest people of the world, many of them the victims of disasters fast (war and weather-related events) and slow (poverty and poor educational and economic opportunities). If ethics has anything to offer the profession and the world, it lies here.

References

Azhar, Gulrez Shah. 2017. "Climate Change will Displace Millions in Coming Decades. Nations should Prepare Now to Help Them." *The Conversation.* December. https://theconversation.com/climate-change-will-displace-millions-in-coming-decades-nations-should-prepare-now-to-help-them-89274. Accessed July 31, 2018.

Hanson, Gladys & Condon, Emmet. 1989. *Denial of Disaster: The Untold Story and Photographs of the San Francisco Earthquake of 1906.* Petaluma, CA: Cameron and Company.

Klein, Naomi. 2007. *The Shock Doctrine: The Rise of Disaster Capitalism.* Toronto: Random House.

NOAA, National Centers for Environmental Information. 2018. *Billion-Dollar Weather and Climate Disasters: Summary Stats. www.ncdc.noaa.gov/billions/summary-stats.*

United Nations. 2018. *World Urbanization Prospects.* https://esa.un.org/unpd/wup/Publications/Files/WUP2018-KeyFacts.pdf. Accessed July 31, 2018.

Chapter 14

Diversity

Like many cities around the world, mine has become increasingly diverse, with sizable Somalian, Ethiopian, and Hmong populations, as well as African American, Indian, Chinese, and Mexican among many others. Cities have long attracted people from far-away places as caldrons for the exchange of goods and the pursuit of economic opportunity, and that has accelerated in recent decades with urban populations swelling as people struggle with impoverished conditions at home and go elsewhere to seek better lives. Which makes diversity a good measure of a city's economic health: the more people from more places who want to live in a place, the stronger its attraction and the more interactions take place there.

The bio-physicist Geoffrey West has argued that this is a matter of scale: the bigger the city, the more cross-pollination of people and ideas, leading to good outcomes – a higher number of patents, greater productivity, rising standards of living – and bad ones: more pollution, growing crime, increased over-crowding (West, 2017). West sees the expansion of cities in our time not just as an economic issue, but a matter of human survival. He sees humanity as having grown our ecological footprint through the use of technology to the point where our species faces collapse unless we can innovate ever faster, which people do in cities far better than when living in isolation. The more we come in contact with people unlike ourselves, the more likely we will come up with new ideas and innovative discoveries.

This work presents an irony for architects. The architectural community has always valued cities, in part because cities have more buildings designed by architects than smaller settlements, but the profession also remains one of the least diverse of all the major professions, with the percentage of people of color often much smaller than their percentage in the general population. Most architects will say they value diversity, but the profession has not practiced what it preaches. That has begun to change: many architecture schools now actively recruit students of color and pupils from across the globe, and the architectural profession has acknowledged its lack of diversity and is seeking remedies for it, however minimal the impact so far. But the reason to seek a more diverse profession goes beyond that of reflecting

Figure 14.1 Big cities, such as Shanghai, China, have more of the good – more efficiency, creativity, and economic activity – as well as more of the bad – pollution, crime, and congestion. Cities remain, though, one of the most resilient of human inventions.

more closely the communities in which architects work. It has to do with the value that architecture and diversity create.

Innovation arises out of diverse populations because of the different paradigms that people bring to an issue as a result of the cultures they come from. The scientist Thomas Kuhn coined the term "paradigm shift" to describe situations when our existing explanations of the facts of some reality no longer align with the evidence and when new concepts remerge that better explain what we see going on. While Kuhn had science in mind when wrote about these new paradigms, his meme has broad applications in the social sciences, arts, and humanities for understanding the different ways in which various cultures explain the world (Kuhn, 2012).

The value of diversity lies here. People from various cultures will have different explanations of the same phenomena, representing different paradigms in how we conceive of the reality around us. Which makes simply adding a person from a different culture or ethnicity not enough if we don't also allow for a deep engagement with their view of the world and their conception of reality. Token diversity misses the real value of difference. We should not look to people from other cultures to fit our constructs and conceptions; instead we should learn from their perspectives and understand their paradigms in order to question our own. Diversity is important not only to give everyone an equal opportunity, but also to allow each of us to see and comprehend what lies around us in completely new ways.

That, I would argue, is what architects also do – or at least should do. The profession thinks of itself as the designers of buildings, but engineers or contractors can do that, however ugly or dysfunctional the results might be. Architects do something just as important: imagining new paradigms, new ways of living and being in the world. From that perspective, the lack of diversity in the ranks of architects makes the real work of the profession more difficult by cutting it off from the range of paradigms that cultures have created and in which lie new solutions to the challenges we face as individuals and as communities of people.

Great cities accommodate those divergent ways of conceiving of the world. Except for those few created out of a dystopian urge for singularity or consistency, such as Hitler's Third Reich, embodied in Albert Speer's plans for Nazi Berlin, cities present the place for difference to occur and for us to see those differences in the behavior and beliefs of the people who embody them. In my city, the Twin Cities of Minneapolis and St. Paul, we have the fortune of seeing two East African cultures, Somali and Ethiopian,

Figure 14.2 Although the city provides the perfect vehicle to counter prejudice through the interaction of diverse people, it can also foment intolerance, as happened in Nazi-controlled Berlin and as continues to happen today in highly segregated cities.

rooted in different religions, Islam and Christianity, and yet similar in the weight that they place on family, piety, and modesty – values at odds with the individualism, skepticism, and extroversion that has come to characterize at least some parts of American popular culture. The city does not force those values on anyone. If anything, healthy urban life teaches us how to tolerate a wide range of people and cultures and to transcend our own ideas about world.

The ethics of Emmanuel Levinas expressed this powerfully. He wrote that, "Morality accomplishes society . . . It is something other than the co-existence of a multitude of humans . . . Society is the miracle of moving out of oneself" (qtd. in Sessler, 2008, p. 28). That idea can help us understand diversity and the city in new ways. We come to cities not just for economic opportunity, but also to experience that "miracle of moving out of oneself," to overcome our individual limits and cultural blinders in order to "accomplish" something greater, to be a part of a larger community: society. And cities enable us to do so not just by letting us co-exist, but also to come face-to-face with the Other, as Levinas often put it, which prompts the kinds of innovations that we need, as a species, in order to thrive going forward. If architecture provides a way to redesign our reality based on these cultural paradigms, cities provide the place in which to cultivate them, and diversity, the nutrients in which they grow and flourish.

References

Kuhn, Thomas. 2012. *The Structure of Scientific Revolutions*. Chicago: University of Chicago Press, 4th ed.

Sessler, Tal. 2008. *Levinas and Camus: Humanism for the Twenty-First Century*. New York: Continuum.

West, Geoffrey. 2017. *Scale: The Universal Laws of Growth, Innovation, Sustainability and the Pace of Life in Organisms, Cities, Economies, and Companies*. New York: Penguin Press.

Chapter 15

Education

Teaching at a university, I am constantly reminded of how the buildings in which I work and the spaces in which I teach reinforce ethical ideas, sometimes in direct conflict with what I believe or seemingly with what students want. This is understandable at one level. Universities, like schools everywhere, have a lot of buildings that they have inherited from the past and still need to use, whether or not these structures function as well as they could or serve the educational needs of the people who occupy them. But at another level, that sunk cost in older buildings has become especially problematic given the transformation in education that has happened with the digital revolution. Students can now get degrees online and can access information faster and often more accurately than a teacher can deliver it, all for a much lower cost than what face-to-face learning demands, and so: why come to a school or campus anymore in order to get an education?

There remain reasons why students should do so, but the reasons have changed. No longer about the conveyance of information, which now happens more effectively through other means, education has become, instead, about conversations, provocations, and interactions not possible in the digital environment, where teacher and student engage in the discovery of new knowledge, in the co-creation of new ideas, and in the serendipitous experiences that can only happen in physical space.

As a result, I have largely stopped lecturing and instead teach in ways that would have seemed strange to the professors who taught me. In one of my courses, we treat the entire campus as our classroom and move around to spaces that my students choose to go. This relates to the topic of the course, on the meaning of space, but it also empowers students to have some agency over where and how they learn, and their choices are telling: rarely do they chose a classroom and instead, they often select places that have comfortable furniture and daylight, within larger spaces that have other people not in the course sitting or walking nearby. My students seem to appreciate having the ability to make this choice about their learning environments and it conveys, in physical form, the responsibility they will need to take about their on-going education throughout their lives, little of which will likely occur in a classroom.

Figure 15.1 Education began outdoors and for most of our history as a species we learned in nature. It is no wonder that, for many students, learning outside of a classroom leads to better retention of the material, by engaging all of our senses.

As their teacher, I have also become their co-learner and co-creator, following them as much as leading them, and improvising with them as we go, carrying a large post-it pad with me, since the places my students select almost never have a screen or white board. From the point of view of ethics, our move out of the classroom and across the campus helps students get into the habit of thinking about the needs of others: what students in the course might require in terms of accommodations and even what I might need to have available, as their teacher, in order to show slides or make notes that all can see. And because the places in which the students choose to learn rarely include a classroom, the course shifts how we think about other spaces – lounges, hallways, stairways, coffee shops – in terms of learning.

Our occupation of these supposedly non-learning spaces also suggests an ethical shift in the power relationships and functional determinacy embedded in the typical classroom. The students often sit in roughly a circle or at a table with me in the middle of the group, which shifts the power relationship from me, the professor, at the front of a traditional lecture hall, with students sitting quietly taking notes, to a more co-equal relationship among us through our arrangement and occupation of the furniture. Other students not enrolled in the class also occasionally listen in on our conversations and sometimes even participate, suggesting that such serendipitous encounters, made difficult in the past with classrooms held in dedicated spaces behind closed doors, may be one of the major reasons why students might want to come to campus, to experience interactions that no digital environment can replicate.

I realize as my students talk about what they learned in the class that the various spaces we occupy also become memory devices for the content of the course. Rather than sit in the same, sterile classroom, with its antiseptic floors, white walls and fluorescent lights depriving students of much sensory stimulation, my students and I have conversations in places with unique smells and sounds, distinct space and light qualities, and diverse types and configurations of furniture, which links the content of what we talk about to the sensual information subconsciously absorbed in the process. Students will often remember an idea or conversation by recalling the place in which we discussed it, turning those learning spaces into a kind of memory palace, similar to those used in medieval education to help students remember information and ideas prior to widespread availability of printed books.

My nomadic course represents one small example of what is ethical about architecture and what architects have to offer ethics. The buildings we occupy every day often force us into relationships that may no longer fit our values or meet our needs, much as the traditional classrooms in which I get assigned to teach no longer make sense to me, given the spatial freedom enabled by mobile, digital devices. We can say the same about retail spaces, whose voluminous spaces and repetitive aisles of goods seems redundant in an era of online shopping; or about large single-family homes, whose sheer size and often distant location no longer fit the needs of smaller families and rising living costs; or about private offices, whose use of space in expensive real estate no long seems appropriate as companies seek more interaction among their employees and flexibility in their operations.

Buildings generally last a long time and change relatively slowly and at great expense, and as a result, they often reflect older values and assumptions that require our adaptation and occasional resistance. This may not have mattered as much in earlier eras, in which many things changed just as slowly, but with change now happening at exponential rates, buildings need to be more accepting of uses and activities that we may not even imagine today. Although the digital world will never replace the bricks-and-mortar one, the latter needs to do what the former can't, including the accommodation of serendipitous, sensual, and immersive experiences that no computer can match and that no building program can easily anticipate.

Too many people see architects as an expense they can't afford or that they want to minimize if they can't avoid it. But that perception often misses the point – one that not enough architects make – about architecture as a value generator, creating social, cultural, financial, and natural capital where it did not exist before. Nor does this happen just with one building

Figure 15.2 The arrangements of spaces and fixed furniture in buildings dictates power relationships, such as those that have traditionally existed between teachers and students and that no longer seem tenable in the era of Internet-connected digital devices.

at a time. As I have learned from the students in my nomadic class, their re-imagining of spaces as places in which to learn and their agency in being able to occupy spaces in new ways, requires an urban fabric that allows for appropriation. Isolating buildings from each other and designing them in ways that only allows a single, narrowly defined use makes no more sense in the twenty-first century than isolating disciplines and ghettoizing them each in their own buildings on campus. If there is one thing to learn from young people today it is that education and innovation demand the crossing of boundaries of all sorts, architectural as well as intellectual.

Chapter 16

Ghettos

I grew up was an affluent ghetto. That may sound like an oxymoron, since we tend to associate ghettos with poor or oppressed people, such as the first ghetto in Venice, Italy, where the government ordered by decree in 1516, that people of Jewish faith live in a single neighborhood, separate from the rest of the city. But as places in which a homogenous population of people live apart from those different from themselves, ghettos come in all flavors, some of them enforced by law, as the one in Venice, and others established through policies, such as the red-lining of certain neighborhoods by banks and real estate agents in the twentieth century, and still others by self-imposed segregation, as happened with at least some of the residents in the town in which I lived.

Self-imposed segregation may not seem as onerous as that imposed upon us. The people in my home-town had the ability to leave if they wanted to, as I did the moment I reached adulthood, while those trapped in poverty and living in segregated communities often do not have that option. But I learned growing up that ghettos exist in the mind as well as in physical places, with the former sometimes as hard to escape as the latter. Like the first ghetto, founded out of Venetian's unfounded fear of Jews, some of my childhood friends spoke of similar fears: of the city that lay just 20 miles away, of the poor who had no easy way to get to my ex-urban hometown even if they had wanted to, and of anyone different from the town's upper- and upper-middle class citizenry, isolated down their long driveways within their acres of trees.

Because of the wealth of that place, many of the homeowners had architects design their houses, some of them modern (if not visible from the road) and most adhering to the community's aesthetic brand as a New England Village knock-off, with gable-roofed wood-framed structures, clad in white clapboarded walls, with shuttered multi-pane windows. This visually uniform fantasy had a peculiar history. It resulted from a group of industrialists who had made their fortunes in the factories of the nearby city wanting a place in which to retreat from the noise, pollution, and poverty generated by their own companies and who took over an old mill town and converted

Figure 16.1 While the imagined New England village of my youth provided a safe and supportive place in which to grow up, it started to feel like a high-end ghetto as I became aware of all who it kept out and kept us from.

it into their Potemkin village in the early twentieth century. While several of the town's founders had New England roots, their imposition of a common architectural style and a strict design-review process ensured that, contrary to actual diversity of many New England towns, no one would disrupt the fiction they had created.

The tragedy of ghettos arises in the limits they place on people's experiences and choices. For the poor or oppressed, those limits have resulted from racial, ethnic, and religious prejudice: bigotry that has become illegal in many places around the world, but not always eradicated, as we have seen with the re-emergence of white supremacy, extreme nationalism, and religiously-driven terrorism. The fight against intolerance is really a fight against all who would limit the opportunities and experiences of others, which no doubt arises from their own limited opportunities and experiences. Ghettos perpetuate ghettos as those who segregate others often segregate themselves. And without a concerted effort to break down the walls of ghettos – be they urban or rural, for the rich or poor, out of fear or prejudice – we will continue to ghettoize ourselves and limit our possibilities in the process.

My upbringing in that ghetto of affluence had a paradoxical quality since the Stoicism of my psychologist father represented an ethical stance completely contrary to the values of many in the community around us. Perhaps the greatest Stoic philosopher, Epictetus, spent much of his life as a Roman slave and had a physical disability that required his use of a crutch. He experienced injustice and prejudice first-hand, and no doubt because of that, he espoused an ethics that recognized the creative drive and human potential in everyone, regardless of their situation in life (Epictetus, 1952). Epictetus did not blame his slave owners or those who discriminated against him because of his infirmity or oppressed position. Instead, he saw how much their intolerance limited their own potential.

My parents lived in that town until my father's death and I can understand why. After a day of listening to and talking with his patients, my father sought refuge in our woods, far from neighbors and whatever psychological issues they might have. And he lived the advice he gave his patients, the Stoic advice to not bother yourself about things beyond your control; my father had no control over the prejudices of some of the residents of our town and he didn't bother himself about them. But as soon as I could, I got

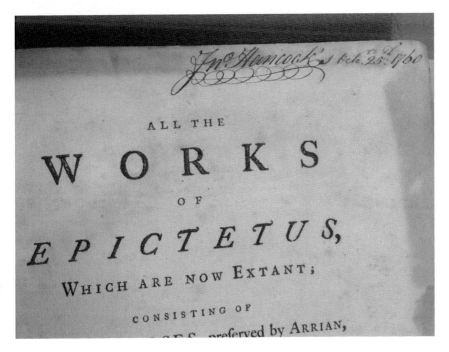

Figure 16.2 The Stoicism of Epictetus had a powerful influence on people prior to the age of instant-gratification consumerism. This copy of Epictetus's work in Harvard's Houghton Library was that John Hancock, the famous signatory of the Declaration of Independence.

out of that ghetto and lived in a variety of very diverse communities. That puzzled some of my colleagues, leading one of them to assume that I had no choice but to live in such places and that I was, as he said, "slumming it." He may have seen my neighborhood as a ghetto, but I came to realize that he lived in one as well, in his own mind.

Those experiences have led me to suspect every effort by people to protect the character or preserve the status quo of where they live. Those who make such claims often forget that what they so jealously want to protect often destroyed the character of what came before: when those industrialists took over the small mill town in which I lived and greatly altered it to look like a New England village, they drove out the much more diverse community that existed there in the nineteenth century. And those who use preservation to stop change often don't stop to think about what bothers them so much about it. Are they bothered by what lies beyond their control, given the inevitability of change, or do they simply want to maintain the self-imposed segregation that insulates them from others? As I watch the self-defeating and often paradoxical preservation battles that some communities continue to wage, I remember a lesson of my youth: the psychological ghettos we construct for ourselves are far more oppressive and much harder to overcome than any of the physical ones that still exist. As Epictetus put it, "It is a man's own opinions which disturb him" (Epictetus, 1952, p. 125).

Reference

Epictetus. 1952. *The Discourses*. Chicago: University of Chicago Press, Vol 12.

Chapter 17

Gifts

My university, like most, has students from all over the world, and sometimes foreign graduate students joining my research center bring gifts as a sign of appreciation or respect. I accept them and put them on my office shelves as a show of my gratitude for their generosity, but these tokens raise the question in my mind of when a gift becomes a way of ensuring preferential treatment or favorable assessment.

An architect I know, who works a lot overseas, has mentioned how common it has become for regulators in certain countries to expect such gifts – if not outright payments – to expedite a review or affect a decision. She said that the developers she has worked for see that as just part of the cost of doing business in such places, knowing that they will have to pay to play. She also has spoken of product vendors who, wanting to influence selection decisions, would send a bottle of wine or liquor to her specifier, who took the view that one bottle constituted a gift, two a bribe.

The codes of ethics in the architectural profession have clear stipulations against the giving or accepting of bribes. The Royal Institute of British Architects code of ethics has a concise statement: "Members should not offer or take bribes in connection with their professional work" (RIBA, 2005). That principle leaves it up to the people involved to determine what represents a bribe, which can be challenging in a global economy, with culturally diverse ways of distinguishing between a gift and bribe.

The American Institute of Architects' code puts more emphasis on intent: "Members shall neither offer nor make any payment or gift to a public official with the intent of influencing the official's judgment in connection with an existing or prospective project in which the Members are interested," and "Members serving in a public capacity shall not accept payments or gifts which are intended to influence their judgment" (AIA, 2017). Proving intent, of course, can be difficult and a great deal of ethical debate hinges on the issue of intention.

Kant famously argued that we cannot know whether or not something is good or bad by looking at the consequences of that action: if a bribe to an official expedites the review of a good building that improves its physical

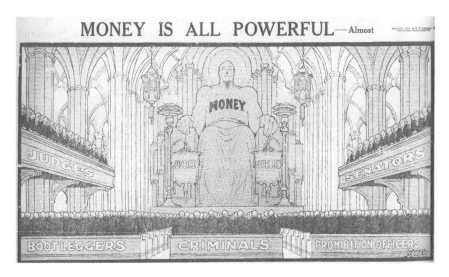

Figure 17.1 As this 1930 Winsor McCay cartoon suggests, money has long provided the place in which many criminals worship, as well as some judges, politicians, police, and even the occasional design professional.

environment, does that make the bribe good? Kant – and the AIA's code of ethics – would say no, since the bribe came with the intention of influencing an official's judgment, however beneficial the results. The challenge, of course, comes in knowing the intentions behind an action: architects, contractors, or vendors giving something of value to an official can claim that they had innocent intentions, that theirs was a gift not a bribe, meant as a token of appreciation not as a way to affect the decision of the person in power.

The terms we use here matter. The RIBA code uses the word "bribe" while the AIA code uses "payments or gifts," with the former based on the assumption that a bribe implies self-serving intent, and the latter, on the assumption that a payment or gift can be well-intentioned or not depending upon the circumstances and the power relations among the people involved. A gift to a colleague who has no power of decision over what we do or to a public official after a decision was made, with no expectation of reciprocity, has a different meaning than one given to influence a relationship or a decision beforehand, so the timing of a gift can matter as much as the intent behind it.

The anthropologist Bronislaw Malinowski first identified what he called a "gift economy" among the indigenous people of the Trobriand Islands in Melanesia (Malinowski, 1922). In such cultures, people exchange gifts with no intention of reciprocity, using gifts to build community and goodwill among potential adversaries. In a market economy, based on payments for goods or services, gifts take on a more complex meaning. Does a present given to a professor by a research assistant or a bottle of wine given to a colleague after a decision is made represent a gift with no expectation of return, or has market economics made human relationships so transactional that we see such offerings as an attempt to influence assessment or judgment, regardless of the intent?

Does the RIBA code recognize that in a way that the AIA code does not? Does the intention behind a gift matter – even if we could prove it one way or the other – if the receiver interprets it as a bribe? In that sense, the RIBA's more direct statement about not giving or taking a bribe expresses the insight that what matters here is interpretation, not intent, and that a gift becomes a bribe if either party sees it as such. Nor does quantity matter here. The idea that one bottle is a gift, two a bribe, may be how that recipient sees it, but if anyone else in the exchange sees even one bottle as a bribe, it becomes so.

Figure 17.2 Whether the giving of something to another person represents a well-intended gift or a favor-seeking bribe depends upon the relationships of the people involved, the timing of the action, and interpretations of it by all involved.

So, what do we do when presented with something like this? Ethical behavior requires what the psychologist Daniel Kahneman calls "slow thinking," in which we should not trust our initial instincts or first responses and, instead, should seek the counsel of others as we deliberate what to do (Kahneman, 2011). Delaying a decision and sharing the responsibility for it can help us arrive at better conclusions, tapping what the writer James Surowiecki has dubbed "the wisdom of crowds" (Surowiecki, 2004). If our colleagues see it as a bribe, then that provides a good measure of how others will likely interpret it as well, and we would do well to not accept it or, if that seems too rude, then to give it away or not use it and put it on a shelf. Gift-giving, of course, takes on a different meaning during certain holidays, when it becomes the norm and more a sign of affection than of influence. But outside of those moments when the market economy overlaps with the gift economy, when a gift has the appearance of a bribe, it is no gift at all.

References

American Institute of Architects, 2017. *2017 Code of Ethics and Professional Conduct*, http://aiad8.prod.acquia-sites.com/sites/default/files/2017-08/2017%20Code%20Update.pdf. Accessed May 21, 2018.

Kahneman, Daniel. 2011. *Thinking Fast and Slow*. New York: Macmillan.

Malinowski, Bronislaw. 1922. *Argonauts of the Western Pacific: An Account of Native Enterprise and Adventure in the Archipelagoes of Melanesian New Guinea*. London: Routledge and Kegan Paul.

McCay, Winsor. 1930. *New York American*.

Royal Institute of British Architects. 2005. *Code of Professional Conduct*. www.architecture.com/-/media/gathercontent/code-of-professional-conduct/additional-documents/codeofprofessionalconductpdf.pdf. Accessed May 21, 2018.

Surowiecki, James. 2004. *The Wisdom of Crowds*. New York: Random House.

Chapter 18

Goodness

I entered architecture school eager to become a practitioner, on a path to work in my family's architectural firm once I graduated, but along the way, I started to encounter questions that both fascinated and perplexed me. How did I know that what I was doing was any good, not just in the sense of getting a "good" grade, but good in the sense of it being useful, relevant, and producing a better future? Eventually, I came to realize that what attracted me to architecture was less the making of buildings and more the creating of a good life for others, which demanded that I understand what a good life entailed and which brought me to ethics, the field that addresses that question most centrally. Many years later, I do not know if I am any closer to answering that question, but I do know that the search has been worth it and a pleasure in and of itself. If nothing else, ethics has helped me see my own field of architecture in new ways.

So how do we know when something – a concept, a design, a building – is any good, not just for those most affected by it, but universally so? Kant believed that for something to be good, it must be so for all people everywhere, and his categorical imperative does provide a kind of universal measure of what most people would consider good: treating other people as ends in themselves rather than as means to our ends and acting as if everything we did were to become the rule for everyone. Reciprocity – doing to others what we would want them do to us – comes perhaps the closest to a universal ethical principle. In architecture, such universal validity has more to do with physics or biology: A structure must be able to withstand gravity, wind, or seismic forces in order to stand up and it must protect people from the elements and insulate us from the heat or cold in order to serve our shelter needs. But beyond that, how far architecture can claim universality remains a question.

Some architects have tried to make such a claim. Consider the architect and educator, and primary author of *A Pattern Language* (1977), Christopher Alexander, whose "pattern language" represents universal patterns of human behavior in physical space and intersubjective responses to the built environment that transcend cultural differences (Alexander,

Ishikawa, Silverstein, et al., 1977). Where those patterns have biological or physical components to them, Alexander has a point: few people would argue against many of these patterns, such as buildings needing to have "good materials" or "efficient structures" or would challenge the idea that all cultures have "sacred sites" or "common land." But Alexander's universality claims become more questionable when his patterns reflect his own Anglo-American background, such as putting the bath, toilet, shower, and basin in a single space, an uncommon combination in many parts of the world. Various cultures use public space, interior space, and the transitions between them differently, and one culture cannot assume that its patterns apply to all. Alexander, to his credit, presents his patterns with some qualification: "The patterns are still hypotheses, all 253 of them," he wrote, "and are therefore all tentative, all free to evolve under the impact of new experience and observation" (Alexander, Ishikawa, Silverstein, et al., 1977, p. xv) Still, the universality of these patterns remains a question.

Kant presented his ethics, like Alexander his patterns, as self-evident, without offering empirical evidence to back them up. The philosopher,

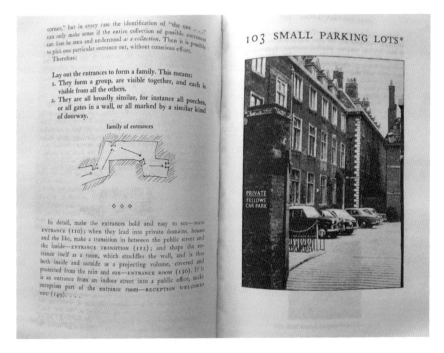

Figure 18.1 While the pattern language has many qualities that most people around the world would understand and embrace, it contains many patterns, like the one about small parking lots, that seems specific to a particular time and place.

Jeremy Bentham, approached this issue more quantifiably, arguing for a utilitarian calculus that assessed the goodness of something according that which creates the greatest good for the greatest number of people. While Bentham's calculus may sound appealing in its promise to put ethics on an measurable footing, how can we ever know what is good for the greatest number unless, of course, we ignore a lot of people and only count those most easily identified, such as those with the greatest money, power, or visibility? And therein lies the paradox of Bentham's utilitarianism: the more implementable it becomes, the more unethical it can also become by reinforcing existing inequalities.

Architects have learned the problems of utilitarianism the hard way. All buildings, of course, have a utilitarian aspect to them in that they have to meet basic functional needs and code requirements, and while that may differ dramatically from one place to another, every building has a degree of utility or it becomes not architecture, but some other form of art, such as sculpture. The fact that buildings must have some utility, though, does not mean that they also must be utilitarian in Bentham's sense of the word. How can any architect know, with any particular design decision, whether it brings the greatest good to the greatest number? It might be possible to calculate that if we take into account only the client and people who will occupy a space, but that leaves out too many others often equally affected by a building: visitors, neighbors, contractors, manufacturers, passers-by, and even future generations. Assessing its impact on all of them becomes practically impossible.

Utilitarianism can also have perverse effects. Take for example a building that accommodates well the needs of everyone who uses it, but that affects only a very few; it might not come close to meeting Bentham's test of providing the greatest good for the greatest number, even if its users consider it a good building. At the same time, a building that has many bad qualities but that serves the needs of a lot of people, is not necessarily a good building, even if it rates higher according to Bentham's calculus. The question is not how many people are affected by something, but who is affected by it and in what way?

More recent philosophers, like Peter Singer, have asked such questions and greatly expanded the scope of utilitarian ethics. Singer has argued that we have to include not just humans, but also animals as equally sentient beings in our calculations of the greatest good, which leads to hugely different results than what most utilitarian solutions would suggest (Singer, 1993). Even if we could determine whether or not a building offered the greatest good for the greatest number of people, the reality remains that many buildings do a lot of damage to their sites in the process of their construction: disrupting soils, displacing animals, and destroying at least some of the property's habitat. And since the number of animals of all sorts above and below ground on a site far exceeds that of the people occupying a building, architecture as we know it now rarely meets the utilitarian calculus as Singer defines it.

But Singer's calculus makes it no easier to measure what constitutes the good than Bentham's, which raises the question of whether the "good" remains beyond our ability to determine it. The philosopher G.E. Moore argued that the good remains a simple un-analyzable topic that we should not try to judge since it cannot be quantifiably measured, rationally argued, or objectively defined (Moore, 1903). His position reflected a larger shift in twentieth-century Anglo-American thought, with its emphasis on logic and scientism, that increasingly viewed the good as a subjective, intuitive, and emotive response to a situation or action, in which anyone's opinion or reaction was just as valid as anyone else. What is good is whatever I say it is, as long as I also acknowledge that my good may not be at all what you think is good.

For the architect, this may sound like both a liberating and debilitating idea. The liberation lies in thinking, that we no longer need to talk about or even care whether or not something is good. It just is, and the only valid assessments of it are those aspects that we can measure and quantify: it's energy performance, say, or its return on investment or its life-cycle cost. That also shows, though, the debilitating nature of relativism: if the good is un-analyzable and not worth discussing, then is it all a matter of one person's opinion rather than another, with the ultimate decision remaining, as Nietzsche argued, with those who have the most power.

Nietzsche viewed goodness differently, as a cover for people's exertion of power (Nietzsche, 2007, p. 69). Because he took a Darwinian view of society, in which the drive to survive defined most human interactions, Nietzsche saw the will-to-power as inherent in human relationships and something to acknowledge rather than fight against, as he saw traditional ethics trying to do. The good, from this perspective, lies with how those in power define it, and equating goodness with virtues such as humility and kindness only empowers those in power even more, enabling them to take advantage of us even further. Better to pull off the mask of false morality and face up to the fact that people have always used the good as a justification for their actions, whatever they might be.

Nietzsche's rejection of traditional Christian ethics reveals a fundamental dilemma for architecture and challenge to any determination of what is, architecturally, good or bad. Buildings are expensive and architects often require their commissioning by people with money or power or both, which places the profession in the difficult position of trying to do good for those who, directly or indirectly, have done some bad things in order to get to where they are. Architecture, to use Nietzsche's analogy, often has to mask the reality that made it even possible. The idea of architecture as an art that reinforces the power of the people who commission or own it, as Nietzsche

Figure 18.2 The Pantheon in Rome captures Nietzsche's sense of architecture as an oratory of power, not only because of the impact of its oculus-lit space, but also because of its representation of the beliefs of those in power, be they pagan or Christian.

wrote, also raises the questions: Is a good building whatever the person or group in power – your professor, your client, a critic – says is good? Does goodness ever inhere in the building itself, or is its goodness just a matter of who gets to make that call in a particular place and time?

Architecture offers, though, another way of thinking about the good that these other ethical arguments only touch upon, because of the tendency among philosophers to develop systems that have universal applicability. Design, in contrast, remains very place-based and scale-sensitive, which means that we must judge the goodness of some aspects of work at the scale of the planet, looking at its effect on all sentient beings; some at the scale of the human community, looking at its biological and physical effects that apply to all people; some at the scale of the culture, looking at its adherence to what a society considers to be good at this time in its history; and some at the scale of the site, looking at what a particular community of people view as acceptable in a particular place. The built environment crosses all of those scales, which means that a work of architecture can be good in some ways and at some scales and not in others. So how do you know if work is good or not? The answer lies in asking another question: good in what way, for whom, and at what scale?

References

Alexander, Christopher; Ishikawa, Sara; Silverstein, Murray; Jacobson, Max; Fiksdahl-King, Ingrid; Angel, Shlomo. 1977. *A Pattern Language: Towns, Buildings, Construction.* New York: Oxford University Press.

Moore, G.E. 1903. *Principia Ethica.* Cambridge: Cambridge University Press. http://fair-use.org/g-e-moore/principia-ethica. Accessed May 21, 2018.

Nietzsche, Friedrich. 2007. *Twilight of the Idols.* Hertfordshire, England: Wordsworth.

Singer, Peter. 1993. *Practical Ethics.* Cambridge: Cambridge University Press.

Chapter 19

Happiness

HGTV – the Home and Garden cable television station – fascinates me more for what it says about us, its viewers, than what it actually shows. Its focus on the buying, building, renovating, and redecorating of houses across the world offers not just a lot of practical advice on how to do such things, but also a voyeuristic glimpse into the ways in which other people live and in which the viewers might want to live if they only had enough time or money. We might think of it not just as a home and garden station, but also as a

Figure 19.1 The Biltmore in Ashville, North Carolina, shows how much houses do not just meet our basic needs, but also become vehicles for conspicuous consumption and status-seeking, activities almost guaranteed to make people unhappy.

happiness grabbing one, letting us imagine ourselves in another place, more pleasurable than the one we currently occupy.

Architecture has long played this pleasure-seeking role. While most people inhabit buildings for practical reasons, to have space in which to live or work and to have a roof over our heads, architecture has also represented something more existential: the pursuit of happiness. As almost every building owner or occupant has considered at some point, we seem inclined to think how much happier we would be if we only had more space, more land, more of a view, and so on. Such pleasure-seeking thinking has also affected ethics. The hedonistic ethics of Jeremy Bentham, for example, assumes that people seek to maximize their happiness and that we can measure the good according to what helps us achieve that maximizing goal.

At the same time, ethics has questioned hedonism as the source of happiness and happiness itself as a goal. Stoic and Buddhist ethics, for instance, argue that our attachment to things and our drive to want more than what we have leads not to more happiness, but its opposite: unhappiness. As the Buddha purportedly said, "Happiness does not depend on what you have or who you are; it solely relies on what you think." If happiness is a state of mind, what does it have to do with the physical world around us?

In his book *Anarchy, State, and Utopia*, the philosopher Robert Nozick asks if we would call people happy if they spent their lives floating in a tank, with electrodes on their skulls attaching them to "experience machines" that constantly simulated pleasurable thoughts and feelings (Nozick, 1974). Most people would respond to Nozick's thought experiment with a resounding no. We might feel happy because of the artificial stimulation of pleasure points in the brain, be it through electrodes or opioids, but most of us would not call such a life a happy one. A happy life does not mean a lack of unhappiness. Indeed, we generally conceive of a happy life as one that has overcome unexpected setbacks, achieved meaningful accomplishments, and entailed a sense of purpose – in other words, some level of unhappiness or at least a degree of challenge or hardship.

That idea has sometimes gotten lost in a consumer culture that has encouraged us to equate happiness with a lack of adversity and a lot wealth, privacy, and material goods, leading among other things to increasingly large homes and a seemingly unceasing pursuit of property. As a result, many people have grown accustomed to seeing happiness as a lack of pain, suffering, or even inconvenience, as if such a life – short of being attached to an experience machine our whole lives – were even possible. We cannot know the meaning of anything without also knowing its opposite or its lack, and so the experience of happiness depends at least to some degree on the experience of unhappiness, which serves as a measure against which we can gauge our transcendence of it.

Architects and designers often confront the unbalanced view of happiness in modern, consumer cultures when dealing with the wealthiest of clients. In a world where inequality has reached record proportions, with a small percentage of people controlling a huge percentage of the wealth, the capability of the super-rich to afford almost anything has become legend. This, in turn, can lead to requests that would have been unbelievable just a couple of generations ago. As the author and university president, Michael Ignatieff, observes in his book *The Needs of Strangers*, Western culture has engaged in a continual upward spiral of needs, in which luxuries in one generation become the norm in later ones (Ignatieff, 1984).

We can track that upward spiral in architecture, where the luxuries of the past – internal plumbing, central heating and air conditioning – have become essential and expected parts of most buildings. And the upward spiral continues, with media rooms and mini-gyms, and multi-vehicle garages increasingly a part of at least high-end homes, enabling their residents to live almost completely autonomously and cut-off from the community around them. Such houses have some of the characteristics of Nozick's "experience machine," able to connect us through electronic means to almost every pleasure imaginable.

But does that constitute happiness? Design professionals – and, indeed, many people – tend to shrug off such a question. Along with our tolerance of intolerable levels of inequality has come a view of happiness as something subjective and as a result, different for each individual. If clients can afford a house like that and it makes them and their family happy, who can argue? Most architects won't, since the larger and more expensive the project, often the higher the design fees. The system encourages over-consumption on the part of both people and the professionals who serve them.

But happiness is not entirely subjective, as we see from Nozick's "experience machine." Most of us can agree on the basic constituents of a happy life – one that includes good relationships with family and friends, a sense of purpose and accomplishment, a sense of health and well-being, and so on. Research has also shown that above a certain level, having more stuff – especially if it comes at the expense of these other values – does not make us happier; if anything, as the Buddha knew, it can make us less so (Haidt, 2006).

For architecture, the ethical question here has more to do with professional responsibility than with personal proclivities. While architects have a duty to respond to a client's needs, the field also has an obligation to meet those needs in as effective, efficient, and environmentally responsible a way as possible, which can include creating spaces that have multiple uses and that demand minimal amounts of energy and materials. This does not require asking the client's permission; it represents professional best practice and the surest route to happiness on the part of the client and the architect alike.

Figure 19.2 Some of the greatest wealth comes through the building of social capital, with events such as outdoor block parties and free street festivals that encourage people to take back the spaces that often divide us.

References

Haidt, Jonathan. 2006. *The Happiness Hypothesis: Finding Modern Truth in Ancient Wisdom*. New York: Basic Books.

Ignatieff, Michael. 1984. *The Needs of Strangers*. New York: Picador.

Nozick, Robert. 1974. *Anarchy, State, and Utopia*. New York: Basic Books.

Chapter 20

Helping others

Like many people in my community, I give a lot of my time to non-profit boards and volunteer activities of various sorts. I don't do this for accolades of any kind; indeed, I rarely tell anyone about this side of my life, in part because when I do, people often think I do too much of it. They may be right, but I do it because it suits the paradoxical way in which the world works: the more we give, the more we get. In that sense, my volunteer work remains both a way of giving and a way of getting back more than I give, even though I have a hard time explaining the latter. Helping others is the best way that I have learned to help myself.

That paradox has deep roots in ethics. The biblical ethic of doing unto others as you would have them do unto you captures this idea of reciprocity, as does John's urging in the Bible that "If you have two shirts, give one to the poor. If you have food, share it with those who are hungry." Although raised a Christian, I am not religious, but I do think that the ethics of Jesus and his followers has real value, as Thomas Jefferson believed when he eliminated the book's overtly spiritual parts and combined the ethical ideas into what became known as the Jefferson Bible (Jefferson, 2015).

Helping others doesn't have to be planned ahead; plenty of opportunities exist right in front of us. I walked outside my office the other day to see a seriously inebriated man attempting to get on his bicycle and nearly falling into a street with passing cars, and not long after that, walking away from a meeting in a local coffee shop, I saw a man in an electrified wheelchair tipped over in a parking lot, with the food in the bag he had carried spilled out across the pavement. In both cases, I had other places to go, but I could not leave them that way. As the philosopher Immanuel Kant argued, we need to do what is right regardless of the inconvenience, and so I did, as did other passers-by as well (Kant, 2016).

I called the police for help with the drunk and stayed with him until they arrived so that he wouldn't get hit by a car or fall over on his bike, while I and a colleague of mine helped the disabled man back up in his chair and gathered his food and got him on his way. In both cases, others stopped to offer help, but I don't think I was the first to come upon them, so there were

Figure 20.1 In cities, the distinction between a tool, like a bike, and a machine, like a car, makes all the difference when it comes to engaging with others. Machines tend to divorce us from each other, while tools make it easier to share and to come to each other's aid.

probably others who did not stop, for whatever reason. I don't blame those who walked by and walked on. Different people have different pressures in their lives and perhaps they all had others needing their time and attention as much as these two men.

I wondered, though, how much the built environment contributes to situations like this. We have constructed a world, at least in the West, that can make the enactment of our daily lives a challenge, with considerable distances to travel, with traffic congestion to deal with, and with too many demands upon all of us, with too little time. We have done this out of a sense of utility, of benefiting the greatest number of people, but the environments we have designed for ourselves also lacks a lot of utility, not benefiting anyone as they have become ever more over-crowded, stress-inducing and unhealthy.

With that has come the odd condition, especially in cities, of living out our lives mostly among strangers. That allows any of us to look the other way and walk on by without consequences, even though city life also exposes us to people with diverse backgrounds and enlarges our understanding of how others see the world. The tipping point between a respect for difference and callous indifference may have mostly to do with the density and intensity of environments we inhabit; too many people too much in our face can lead us to not see what is right in front of us, including the occasional person in real need.

Indifference might also come from the insularity of the modern city, with so many of us spending so much of time in private automobiles commuting between private homes and offices. It not only becomes more difficult to stop and help a person when we have to look for a parking space, but also less of a habit when we spend so little time as pedestrians ourselves. And the spaces we have created for our car-acculturated cities can isolate those in need, as was especially the case with the man in the tipped over wheelchair. He lay in a parking lot, between a parked car and a planted berm, largely invisible to anyone not on foot. The city designed for the convenience of many becomes incredibly inconvenient for a few – a tyranny of the majority, as the author Alexis de Tocqueville called it, that a majority rarely acknowledge or even see (De Tocqueville, 2004).

Can the built environment change this situation? At one level, maybe not, since the places we create reflect what we value, even if we don't recognize

Figure 20.2 The tragedy of car-dominated landscapes lies in their keeping us physically close and psychologically remote, leaving us unable or unwilling to help each other because of our own sense of isolation.

that mirroring effect or like what we see in the mirror. But at another level, the physical environment absolutely has this power to change things, by making it faster to walk places than to drive, easier to help those in distress than to pass them by, and better to acknowledge strangers than to ignore them. The physical environment, of course, cannot force us to do any of this; it cannot make us moral if we have no habit, as Aristotle would say, of being so (Aristotle, 1952). But architects can get the barriers out of the way and put in place the context that makes that habit easier to acquire and act upon, whether that be through volunteering when we can or aiding others when we must. This suggests that we create not just walkable communities, but also communities that allow us to walk in someone else's shoes.

References

Aristotle. 1952. *Nicomachean Ethics*. Chicago: University of Chicago Press, Vol. 9.
De Tocqueville, Alexis. 2004. *Democracy in America*. New York: The Library of America.
Jefferson, Thomas. 2015. *The Jefferson Bible: The Life and Morals of Jesus of Nazareth*. New York: Scriptura Press.
Kant, Immanuel. 2016. *The Collected Works of Immanuel Kant*. London: Delphi Classics.

Chapter 21

Housing

A graduate student and I have been working with doctors and service designers on a way to build housing for the homeless at a massive scale (Clowdus et al, 2018). This work originated in the health community, which has realized that without proper housing, people cannot achieve good health, and that the healthcare system simply cannot sustain or afford the cycle of homeless people in, out, and back in the emergency rooms of hospitals. My medical colleagues recognize that housing equals health and they have set, as their goal, the ability to prescribe housing for a person about to be discharged from the ER who has no place to go.

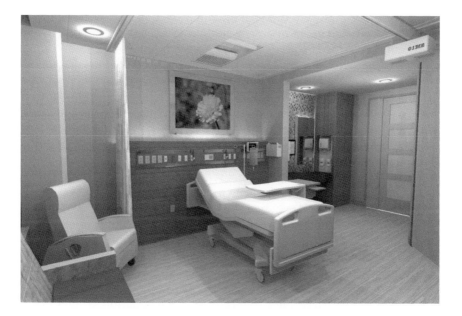

Figure 21.1 We accept patient rooms the size of a "tiny home" in a hospital setting, but many places prohibit the equivalent-sized space when defined as a dwelling, showing the difference we make between health as a right and housing as a responsibility.

I find the commitment of my colleagues inspiring. At the same time, our work has made me wonder about the difference in, and basic unfairness of, public perceptions of health and housing. Most people – and the policy makers who represent them – see health as a right. While that has not translated in some countries, such as the United States, to universal health insurance or a single-payer, government-provided system, it does mean that in most places around the world, hospitals cannot turn away a person in need of medical attention, whether or not they can pay for those services. Some countries, again like the US, interpret that right as access to acute care, not to health per se, and so they spend less much money on keeping people healthy than they do on healing them when sick or injured. Still, health, broadly defined, remains something most of us see as our due.

Not so housing. The fact that so many homeless or poorly housed people exist around the world – living on the streets, occupying informal settlements, moving among refugee camps – shows that we view housing not as a right, but instead as something that separates the haves from the have-nots, those who can afford increasingly costly accommodations from those who cannot. Hospitals will not turn us away if we need care, but unless we have some prior relationship with them, homeowners and landlords will, and they have every right to do so. Property, not housing, remains a right in many countries and that gives property owners discretion in terms of who they house. In most countries, they cannot discriminate based on a person's ethnicity, for example, but they can discriminate according to the ability of that person to pay the rent or afford the mortgage.

Morality plays a part here. We have a long history of seeing health as something that happens to us, over which we have no control, despite the fact that a lot of ill health stems from the poor decisions of people who smoke, over eat, or otherwise do dangerous things. Meanwhile we tend to see housing as something that remains an individual responsibility over which we supposedly have control. As a result, unlike the poor health decisions of people, those who cannot pay for housing sometimes triggers a moralistic response from those who can, evidence of a person's weakness, laziness or recklessness.

That may stem from a time when most people did, indeed, have a great deal of control over their own housing. For most of human history, people built their shelter from what they had at hand – igloos out of ice, tepees out of animal hides, adobes out of sun-dried mud, and huts out of wattle-and-daub. In many parts of the world, though, that no longer happens. We have professionalized housing, as we have healthcare, and taken these activities out of the hands of most people, which has improved the quality of both, but which has not changed the moral equation around them. How can we view housing as our personal responsibility when most places around the world have taken that responsibility from most people in the form of building codes, zoning regulations, and professional licenses?

With the professionalization of medicine, the health community has ensured access to care by developing insurance systems and governmental subsidies that enable hospitals to treat whoever comes through their doors. The professionalization of housing has no equivalent. While some governments around the world have taken on the responsibility of building housing for those who cannot afford it, the quantity, quality, and pace of that construction rarely matches the need. Waiting lists remain long in most places and units themselves often remain below standard, if not outright unsafe, in sometimes unsavory surroundings. People in a given place will go to the same hospital, but they will go home to very different housing, if they have housing at all.

At the core of every licensed profession lies virtue ethics. With the advantage that licensure provides comes the responsibility to perform what Aristotle called the cardinal virtues of courage, justice, temperance and prudence: to do the right thing in the face of wrongs, to ensure fairness where it doesn't exist, to embrace self-control rather than self-interest, and to act wisely when others don't (Aristotle, 1952). And the time has come for the architectural community and the construction industry more broadly to take responsibility for the homeless. This does not just mean designing affordable housing or even devising tiny homes for homeless people; such things remain either too expensive to build in numbers anywhere near the actual need or too much of an exception to the housing system as it currently exists.

We need a new system of housing as extensive as that which we have for health. If people can no longer build whatever shelter meets their needs because of our professionalization and regulation of that process, then we must provide shelter for whoever needs it. And that has to be more than a mattress on the floor of a homeless shelter; it must meet such basic human needs as privacy, security, and safety – none of which exist in group shelters. At the same time, it does not have to be what the regulators would live in. I have heard repeatedly from public officials or planning staff that they would not live in and thus would not approve what homeless people have told us they want: a roof over their heads, walls to keep them warm and give them privacy, a door with a lock, a window they can open, a bed and a place to store their stuff. This may not sound like housing to those comfortably housed, but for those who live on the streets or in a group shelter, it represents the essential elements of home.

Having the courage to do what is right in the face of so much unfairness when it comes to housing and developing a system that ensures that everyone has access to a decent place to live, regardless of their ability to pay, remains a defining moment for the architectural profession. Either it needs to do what the medical community has done to ensure access to healthcare, or step aside and let doctors do what architects have so far failed to do: provide housing for everyone coming through the health system who

Figure 21.2 While high-density housing remains the most efficient way to provide affordable housing, it still takes away the agency of individuals and families to build their own shelter, something that should remain everyone's right to do.

needs it. Housing must become as much of a basic human right as health, since we cannot have one without the other.

References

Aristotle. 1952. *Nicomachean Ethics*. Chicago: University of Chicago Press, Vol. 9.

Clowdus, Gabrielle; Walsh, William; Dempsey, Samantha; Brown, Andrea; Pryor, John; Fisher, Thomas. 2018. "Remote Care Communities for the Chronically Homeless," *Housing and Society*. March. www.tandfonline.com/doi/abs/10.1080/08882746.2018.1439648.

Chapter 22

Inequality

Harold Fisher, my grandfather and an architect of religious buildings for a variety of faiths, once told me that he liked doing such buildings because they were one of the few that anyone could enter and in which all were welcome. I remember admiring the nobility of that sentiment and also the irony of it, since the religious buildings he designed were all very expensive affairs, built with the dollars of wealthy donors. At the time, I recall thinking of my grandfather, and to some extent all architects, as professional Robin Hoods,

Figure 22.1 While temples and churches primarily serve a religion's rituals, such buildings also provide a free and open space in the city, a virtue captured in this drawing of a church by my grandfather, Harold Fisher, in 1949.

"stealing" from the rich, in the form of his donor-dependent architecture, in order to give to the poor, in the form of creating spaces open to all.

That Robin-Hood idea might also serve as a model for how the world deals with the growing economic inequality. The US, for example, has become one the most unequal countries among the developed nations and even among many much-less wealthy countries. At the same time, with that rising inequality has a come a widening political polarization not just in the US, but around the world. While that polarization takes slightly different forms in different countries, the general outline of it remains the same: many people – often in rural areas – feel left behind in a rapidly changing economy, while a few – often in thriving cities – continue to profit enormously from those changes. This has led to other, paradoxical effects. While one might assume that those doing poorly would want more government help, and those doing well, less involvement, the opposite often occurs: some of the strongest advocates for greater equality are themselves wealthy and beneficiaries of the inequality, while many of the loudest opponents to higher taxes come from the ranks of those who would benefit from the social programs they seem to despise.

I have wondered, as I listen to these political debates, what my grandfather would have thought about them. Although not a particularly religious person, he clearly admired religious ethics, which, regardless of the sect, have many traits in common: charity toward those who have less, forgiveness of those who act out of ignorance, faith in the power of human kindness, and love of those who may lack it in their own lives. Modern-day politics would benefit a lot from the ethics of faith traditions, especially those who claim to be believers and yet demonstrate the most uncharitable, unforgiving, and unloving behavior toward anyone who might disagree with them. Like my grandfather's religious architecture, religious purists seem beset with paradoxes that go unrecognized and definitely unacknowledged.

Architects remain caught in this political endgame. As I learned from my grandfather, who avoided all political talk, the costliness of buildings means that most architectural commissions come from wealthy individuals and organizations, as well as from governments and non-profit entities. Architects may not agree with their clients, but the former do have to find ways to get along with the latter in order to get needed buildings built. And yet architects' dependence upon the wealthy for work also means that practitioners must sometimes work for those who may actively oppose efforts on the part of the government to improve the quality of life of the very people who will use or occupy the environments that architects design and whose quality of life architects seek to improve.

Architects can, of course, determine the kind of practice they want to have, and can decide not to work for those whose values or political beliefs run counter to what the profession seeks to achieve. Here personal and professional ethics can collide. The architectural profession, like all such fields, has an obligation to meet the physical and spatial needs of clients or communities, regardless of their political leanings, although I have also known architects to turn down work from those with whom they disagree. Architects also have a responsibility to open up people's thinking about the world around them and how they might see and occupy it differently. Although my grandfather's architecture did not determine what congregants thought or believed, his churches and temples did provide places where people of many different backgrounds and capacities could come together and engage in a shared observance of what transcends us as individuals.

Ethics can help when we face situations like this by redefining the terms of what we consider to be a good life. Most ethical traditions recognize that wealth takes many forms and that the personal satisfaction and social recognition that comes with dedicating ourselves to something we believe in can more than compensate for whatever monetary returns and material rewards may result. This, in turn, reframes how we might think about inequality. So often the debate around this issue assumes that some people have too much – economically, materially, opportunistically – and others too little of the same, and that the ethical path requires helping those who have little get more.

But what if the terms of that debate miss the point? Real equity should lead us to question our assumptions that lead to inequality to begin with. Consider the controversies surrounding the nature and use of public restrooms. Codes in many countries require that women have more fixtures in their restrooms than men, showing how equity requires that we recognize innate human differences. And transgender equity, in turn, has led us to ask why we have gender-specific restrooms at all, rather than fully private toilet stalls that everyone can use, regardless of gender, providing not only equal treatment, but also greater flexibility in who can use these facilities. We all have different needs and accommodating them in as ethically fair and humane a way as possible represents real equity, something my grandfather experienced early in his life.

Orphaned as a child, he never forgot the experience of being abandoned by his parents and beaten by the orphanage director, while the government did nothing to protect him or the others in that brutal institutional setting. My grandfather survived that abuse and was eventually placed in the foster care of a church architect, Ray Fulton, and his family, who had lost their son in World War I. Fulton treated my grandfather like a son, taught him how to be an architect starting at the age of 17, and employed him until the Great Depression forced Fulton to close the office. Architecture, my grandfather used to say, saved his life, and while I think his drive and determination had a lot to do his eventual success as an architect, I do think he had a point.

Figure 22.2 The equal treatment of people, regardless of their gender and orientation, creates better conditions for everyone. Equity does not just benefit a few; it benefits us all since we all have different needs at different points in our lives.

What it took to create the many churches and temples he designed over his 80-some years in practice is what it took for him to live through his orphan years: a lot of faith and hope, with an equal amount of charity and love from others.

Chapter 23

Infrastructure

My first extended conversation with the one of the most perceptive public intellectuals of our time, the architect Rem Koolhaas, took place as I sat in his car and he drove at great speed across Holland's countryside, visiting as many of his projects in as short a time as possible. During that trip, as we raced across the roads of the Netherlands and roamed among the dikes of the Dutch landscape, he spoke about the importance of infrastructure and how, in many ways, it was more important than architecture, a point that

Figure 23.1 Architect Rem Koolhaas and his firm OMA have consistently pointed out architecture's complicity with the forces that undermine it and its dependence upon infrastructure that rarely receives adequate investment.

has remained with me as my own interests have gravitated more toward the systems that support our built environment than the buildings themselves.

While I don't know if infrastructure is truly more important than architecture, I do know that the former lacks the sensitivity that the latter has learned, often the hard way, about matters of culture and context. In their engineer-emulation phase, many modern architects imposed their grand plans on people with little regard for the uniqueness of each place, but after a century of conflict with communities, most architects now acknowledge that the imposition of their vision on others rarely works and always generates an understandable resentment. Some of those who design our infrastructure need to come to the same realization.

An example of this occurred in my area when a public utility planned to run high-tension lines next to a college containing a number of important works of architecture. The power poles and wires would run right in front of the campus and obstruct the view of people as they approached its main entrance. The utility claimed that that location had the lowest cost, but the college took the utility to court to stop the installation of the lines, claiming that the infrastructure would damage the campus and people's perception of it.

As publicly regulated companies, utilities should have the interests of the public uppermost in mind, but conflicts about what constitutes the public's best interest seem embedded in the very word "utility." Ethically, utility means the usefulness of an action, and it leads us to ask, of any situation: did it produce good consequences or bad, and if so, for whom and how many? Utilitarianism, one of the dominant modes of modern ethics, has "utility" as its root word, and it can prove useful in sorting out conflicts like this one.

Among the various types of utilitarianism, the distinction between hedonistic and ideal utility might shed the most light here. Hedonistic utilitarians judge the consequences of an action according to the pleasure it brings or the pain it avoids. In the case of this power utility that wanted to route its lines in the most cost-effective way, the reduced expense to the company and presumably the reduced rate increases to customers that result from it, seemed to produce the most pleasure, if measured economically.

Ideal utilitarians see things differently. They argue that we determine something to be good or bad for reasons that transcend simply pleasure or pain. A good consequence for an ideal utilitarian would factor in intellectual, aesthetic, or even spiritual values, and not just those related to physical pleasure or economic profit. That distinction has obvious relevance to current political debates.

Those who would willingly cut government spending on what they see as extraneous activities in order to keep taxes as low as possible clearly fall into the hedonistic camp, even though such "conservatives" might not like being branded as such. Meanwhile, those who willingly pay more taxes in order to support public benefits such as parks, schools, and arts and cultural organizations just as clearly fall into the idealist camp, a description that might also rub some "liberals" the wrong way.

In the case of those power lines, the power company made a hedonistic argument: run the lines along the lowest-cost route to keep ratepayers' increases down. Meanwhile, the college made an idealist one: the aesthetic value of its buildings made their visual disruption by power lines an unacceptable consequence. These two positions may seem irreconcilable, but not so, according to the nineteenth-century philosopher, John Stuart Mill. He argued for a middle ground: while pleasure matters to people, there are higher and lower pleasures (Mill, 1952). The pleasures of the body and the profits of marketplace, for example, remain of lower quality than the pleasures of the mind and profits of cultural activities, which Mill saw as having a more enduring and ultimately more satisfying nature.

To the utility's hardheaded CEO or to a hard-hearted conservative, such sentiments may seem cloying. When the bottom line becomes the primary determinant of value, intellectual, aesthetic, and spiritual values have little to do with the utility of an action. But ideal utilitarians and those who accept Mill's middle ground have a compelling case here. The slightly increased cost of re-routing the power lines cannot compare to the irreparable damage

Figure 23.2 Some of the best architecture references the infrastructure that underpins it. This Marcel Breuer's building at St. John's University in Collegeville, Minnesota, has glass walls shaded by screen walls made up of clay-tile drainage pipes.

to the college's campus or the visual disruption of peoples' approach to it that the intended location of the power lines would cause.

The rate increase that might come as a result of routing the lines would affect only the ratepayers and only as a one-time charge, while the impact of the proposed route would affect the college's faculty, staff, students, and visitors for a very long time. Based on the simple utilitarian calculus of what brings the greatest good to the greatest number, apart from one's hedonistic and idealistic leanings, there is no question that the greatest utility stemmed from the utility moving its lines and respecting the approach and aura of the campus. The college won the argument and the utility routed its lines in another direction.

The same arguments apply to architecture as well as infrastructure. A client with a hedonistic utilitarian bent might want the lowest-cost and most-familiar building possible, with the goal of minimizing their economic pain and maximizing their aesthetic pleasure. But architects, like communities, need to keep Mill's position in mind: personal hedonistic pleasures rank lower than cultural and community values and responding to the latter will, in the end, lead to a more enduring and ultimately more satisfying result.

Reference

Mill, John Stewart. 1952. *Utilitarianism*. Chicago: University of Chicago Press. Vol. 43.

Chapter 24

Insider information

Like most professionals, architects handle a lot of confidential information and ethics requires that it remain so until – or if – clients approve its release. But the ethics get more complicated when the information involves not a specific project or client, but an organization and the way in which it operates. I once knew an architect who worked for a governmental agency that reviewed and approved architectural projects and who left to become a consultant to clients seeking approvals from the very same agency. While the architect violated no policy or law in using his insider information about the agency on behalf of his clients, some of his former government colleagues thought that his actions violated the confidentiality of his previous employer.

Professional ethics often revolves around the tension between society's assumption that professionals will keep the public interest uppermost in mind and clients' expectation that we will look after their needs first. In many cases, these divided loyalties align and professionals meet the desired outcomes of both their clients and the community. However, when a conflict arises, professionals have to decide where to draw the line and to seek a reasonable resolution.

In the case of this former government employee, his knowledge of how the agency works can make the approval process go more smoothly for both sides, making sure that the agency has the information it needs in order to make a timely decision, which of course benefits the client, too. However, there also exists the possibility that the architect will use that knowledge to help clients push to the limit what the agency will accept and even skirt requirements for which there remains room for interpretation.

The AIA's code of ethics alludes to this possibility with rules such as: "A Member shall not render professional services if the Member's professional judgment could be affected by responsibilities to another project or person, or by the Member's own interests, unless all those who rely on the Member's judgment consent after full disclosure" (AIA, 2017, p. 3) In this case, the architect has fully disclosed his former government employment to clients, who no doubt commissioned him in part because of it. But this situation does raise questions about the architect's divided loyalties. Does he retain a sense of responsibility to his former employer, which might disadvantage his clients, or feel responsible to his clients and so possibly do a disservice to the public interest that the governmental agency seeks to protect?

A related rule in the AIA code of ethics suggests another potential problem with this situation. "Members shall not knowingly disclose information that would adversely affect their client or that they have been asked to maintain in confidence" (AIA, 2017, p. 3). Here, the architect has confidential information about how the agency works and makes decisions as well as confidential information about what his clients intend in terms of meeting – or not meeting – the requirements the agency tries to enforce. The non-disclosure rule in the AIA Code of Ethics, however, expects architects to reveal something held in confidence that might be unlawful or a violation of a legislated policy or judicial ruling. Knowing what the law allows or doesn't allow remains the competitive advantage of this architect, although he treads a fine line between the government seeking to enforce the law and clients who might try to shirk it.

The American Bar Association specifically prohibits attorneys from "represent(ing) a client in connection with a matter in which the lawyer participated personally and substantially as a public officer or employee, unless the appropriate government agency gives its informed consent, confirmed in writing, to the representation" (American Bar Association, 2016). The architectural profession would do well to institute a similar rule. At stake is the public's faith in our ability to keep the public interest in mind, without which we cease being a profession.

A related issue involves consulting firms who join more than one design team competing for the same commission. Each competitor wants the consulting firm on its team because of the expertise it brings to the project, and the presence of the consulting firm on several teams gives it an advantage, increasing the chances that it will win the commission. But the firm's presence on several teams also raises ethical issues related to the privacy, confidentiality, and impartiality toward its multiple partners – a kind of professional polygamy.

Anthropologists have observed that polygamy arises in cultures where maximizing offspring has clear survival value or where there exist a small number of men in relation to women. Such situations, however, remain relatively rare and even in cultures that once accepted polygamy, such as the Mormons, they often move toward monogamy once they have achieved a degree of security and relative equity in the number of men and women. The same seems to exist in professional settings. A consulting firm may find itself wooed by a number of competitors, although the latter may eventually acquire that expertise in-house and have a more monogamous relationship inside the office family than a polygamous one outside of it.

Figure 24.1 Ethics requires that we keep confidences even among family members, as when Eero Saarinen's design won the Gateway Arch competition over the design of his father, who shared the same office.

But polygamy demands a degree of discretion, and when a consulting firm has a similar relationship with several competitors for a project, confidentiality becomes paramount. Some consulting firms put different staff members on different teams to minimize the potential of violating confidential information, even accidentally, among them, although that can create other challenges endemic to polygamy, such as jealousy. What if one team thinks another team got the better or more experienced members of the consulting firm or what if the consultants think one team has a real advantage over others and a greater likelihood of winning the commission? Should the consulting firm put its best people on that team it thinks most likely to win or should the firm, instead, treat even a likely winner the same as every other team, with equally strong people on all of them?

Ethics seems divided on such questions. Duty ethics urges us to treat others equally, as ends in themselves and not means to our ends, while utilitarian ethics asks that seek the greatest good for the greatest number, which if applied to the fortunes of this consulting firm, suggests that it should try to pick winners. The similarity of this situation to marital polygamy suggests otherwise, however. Those who live with multiple marital partners have spoken about the necessity of treating each partner as equally and fairly as possible in order to reduce the potential of jealousy, fear, and anger among them. Ultimately, acting with reciprocity in mind may provide the best course: treat others as you would want to be treated, and handle other's confidential information as you would want them to handle yours.

References

American Bar Association. 2016. *Model Rules of Professional Conduct. www.americanbar.org/groups/professional_responsibility/publications/model_rules_of_professional_conduct/model_rules_of_professional_conduct_table_of_contents.html.* Accessed May 21, 2018.
American Institute of Architects. 2017. *Code of Ethics and Professional Conduct.* Washington DC: AIA.

Chapter 25

Interviews

I once heard a well-known architect start an interview with the comment that the problem with architecture was that he had to convince selection committees, who often know little about the field, to commission him so that he could pursue his art. Sitting on that committee, I cringed at that comment and I was not surprised when other committee members used it as a reason not to give him the commission, but his observation made me think about the particular challenges architects fact in getting work. While every private-sector concern has to compete for work, most sell an established suite of products, a standard set of services, or a well-honed skillset. Architects have the additional challenge of often needing to address a client's unique concerns without knowing much about it at the time of the interview. From my years serving on selection committees, I have been impressed by the number of architects who do this amazingly well. Many have perceptive observations about the clients' situation, while some, like that architect who wanted only to pursue his art, crash and burn on the first sentence.

In the best interviews that I have seen, the architects talk relatively little about themselves and almost entirely about the client and the physical, professional, or political context in which they exist. This shows a practical side to ethics. When we make it a habit to see the world from the perspective of others and think more about their needs than our own, we begin to experience success in the world. This goes contrary to the dominant cultural construct of the "me" generation, in which a focus on one's self provides the path to happiness, and it runs against the grain of marketplace competition, in which touting one's own abilities over others has become almost expected.

But sitting on so many selection committees, I began to see how self-defeating these self-referential habits have become. When every competitor talks about themselves, they all start to sound and look alike, so much so that non-specialists in these selection processes often latch onto some irrelevant feature – the height of one member of a team, the nervousness of another – just to tell them apart. When people mainly talk about themselves, we learn little from such conversations and remember even less.

Figure 25.1 While the architectural community can discern the differences among the work of various architects, selection committees often have a hard time, with a lot of the modern built environment seeming very similar.

Those who do the best in terms of receiving commissions come to the interview having thought deeply about the dilemmas the client faces and bringing to the conversation insights about the situation or possibilities in the projects that even the client had not considered. In those cases, the client often wants to hire that firm to learn more about themselves or to pursue a course that might provide more fruitful than the one they are on. Here, ethics works in the other direction as well. Clients start to see their own world through the eyes of others and many understandably want to continue that process by giving that firm the commission.

Some clients go even further and purposefully set up a situation that challenges the competitors' ethics. An architect told me about an interview in a Middle Eastern country in which the client displayed the presentation materials of all of the architects in the same room, which were visible to each other during the interviews. At the same time, the architects competing for the commission had to wait in an adjacent space with each other and within earshot of each other's interviews, which clearly gave the later competitors an advantage over those who went before them.

The lack of privacy those architects faced in that interview seemed particu-larly ironic since, among the many functions of architecture, one of the most important involves the creation of visual and auditory privacy. Architects create discreet spaces for people so that we can go about our daily activities without worrying about unwanted eavesdropping or undesired snooping on the part of others. And one of modern architecture's signature failures has to do with open spaces that offer little or no visual or auditory separation. While most architects' offices have relatively open floor plans because of the need for collaborative studio space, there remains a need in even the most-participatory workplace for some visual and auditory separation.

So why did the client in this case not grant that to the architects inter-viewing for the commission? It is possible that the client wanted to make a point: either that privacy didn't matter to him or that it did and he wanted to drive that point home by making the architects experience the lack of it. At the same time, this particular client, from a non-Western culture, might have had different view of privacy. In cultures where people often live in

Figure 25.2 Shigeru Ban's Naked House represents one extreme of the open plan, in which the only visual privacy exists inside the large, room-sized cabinets that sit within a single space. This reveals the paradox of freedom: too much of it can be as debilitating as too little.

cramped quarters or in settings without separate rooms for sleeping, for example, people can have an extraordinary ability to block out what they should not see or hear. They have psychological walls and doors equivalent to the physical ones so necessary in most Western countries.

Which brings us to the ethical dilemma of the Western architects competing for this commission. Should they have excused themselves from listening to their competitors and left the room to give their colleagues the privacy that they might have wanted themselves? Should they have accepted the situation and stayed, but actively not listened to their competitors' presentations and not looked at their competitors' boards? Or should they have taken full advantage of the circumstances and altered their presentations to have a competitive edge over their colleagues?

Western ethics offers a clear answer to this: if you would not want others to take advantage of you, you should not do so to them, and so the third option of using a situation to get a competitive edge over others, while possibly economically advantageous, is ethically wrong. More to the point, it is self-defeating, for once architects get known for taking advantage of colleagues, the most valuable asset they have – their reputation – can quickly disintegrate in the opinion of others.

Of the other two options – leaving the room or consciously not listening to the other presentations – the right thing to do depends upon the collegiality of the competitors. They could agree, as a group, to stay and carry on their own conversations among themselves, drowning out the sound of each other's presentations and so creating auditory privacy where it didn't exist in fact. Or, if they could not agree, the right thing – the ethical thing – for each architect to do if feeling ill-at-ease with the situation would be to leave the room until one's time to present. That, of course, might put the architects who leave the room at a competitive disadvantage over those who stay and listen, but maybe not. Often in a such a situation, the advantage lies with those who do not do what others do. And, given the lack of sensitivity of this client to the comfort level of his prospective architects, not getting this commission might have been the best result of all.

Chapter 26

Licensure

I urge my students to get their architectural licenses if they can, since it will give them the greatest opportunities in the work world, able to form their own firm, for example, if they so choose, without the need to depend on other licensed professionals to sign documents for them. While I see this as part of my duty as a professor, I also have misgivings about licensure, especially when it gets used not only as a measure of a person's readiness to practice, but also as a way to keep others from practicing for reasons that seem self-interested.

Professions have long seen licensure as distinguishing them from other commercial enterprises, indicative of the years of training and specialized knowledge that professionals must command. Licensure gives the person who holds it the right to practice. But with rights come responsibilities and here, ethics comes into play: licensure also means that professionals have an obligation to attend to the interests not only of the clients who pay for the architect's services, but also of the general public: those who will directly experience the results of a professional's work and those affected by it only indirectly in some far-away place or in some future time.

Although such shibboleths may sound straightforward, complexities arise when two professions vie for the same turf, which has happened in the US as architects have battled with interior designers over the latter's attempts at becoming a licensed profession. While the opinion of architects on this matter varies considerably, the architectural community as a whole has argued that interior designers should not become a licensed profession. Meanwhile, many interior designers have portrayed that opposition as little more than turf protection, combined with a degree of condescension and gender bias on the part of a predominantly male profession toward a pre-dominantly female one.

This stand-off highlights the contradictions that can occur when a field operates as both a profession and a commercial activity. The American jurist, Wesley Hohfeld argued that rights are duties viewed from another perspective and that our duties differ depending upon what rights we are talking about (Hohfeld, 1978). Professions, for example, have a duty

Figure 26.1 Modern architecture has long blurred the boundaries between architecture, landscape architecture and interior design, as Le Corbusier's Villa Savoye shows, with outdoor and indoor rooms and landscape inside and outside the house's walls.

to prevent those who lack the proper qualifications from practicing by upholding licensure laws, and yet when that duty stems from a desire to suppress a legitimate competitor, the profession has no right to do so and moreover, has a duty to refrain from such anti-competitive behavior. The case against interior designers' licensure has to make a viable case that it would endanger public health, safety and welfare.

The architectural community has given as an example the possibility that interior designers, if licensed, could team up with engineers and design a building without ever involving an architect. While this might result in some ugly buildings, architects have not made the case that such a pairing – even if it ever happened – would endanger the public, and so this argument seems like a blatant anti-competitive position of not wanting interior design/engineering alliances to reduce the amount of work going to architects. To use Hohfeld's logic, architects have no right to make such a claim – certainly without ample evidence to back it up – and have, instead, a duty to refrain from it.

Another challenge comes from the fact that other building-related fields such as engineering and landscape architecture are licensed, something that the architectural community has long accepted. Architects depend upon those other fields for the specialized knowledge they bring to projects, expertise that building designers may not have. But when the work overlaps with what architects do, as is the case with interior designers, the former have fought off the latter, arguing that any effort to define the difference between their respective responsibilities becomes impossible. Further, architects have claimed that since they already have legal responsibility for the entire building, inside and out, licensing interior designers becomes unnecessary and redundant.

Yet here too, the argument sounds simply self-serving. Electrical, mechanical, and structural engineers, for example, often work extensively on the inside of buildings and architects have not questioned the legitimacy of engineers' licenses. Why then do architects question the expertise of interior designers whose knowledge of furniture, fixtures, and finishes often extends far beyond that of most architects?

This dispute has become more heated as the global economy has increased competition between the two fields. As design services have become readily available from almost anywhere around the world, the urge to protect one's turf becomes ever stronger as free-trade fervor seeks to override all such protections. This has led, in the case of interior design licensure, to the decidedly odd situation of libertarian groups opposed to professional licensure joining licensed architects trying to prevent their interiors colleagues from becoming so. How long will it take before these same libertarian groups to turn on architects? As Aesop famously said, we often give our enemies the means of our own destruction.

While politics has dominated the battle over interior design licensure, ethics may offer more help in sorting out which of the antagonists in this situation have right on their side. Both architects and interior designers have claimed to have the best interests of the public in mind when defending their positions, but when we consider what would bring the greatest good to the greatest number of people, it becomes hard to support either side, since internecine war between two professions does a lot of damage to the reputation of both and very little to help anyone else.

If anything, the growing belief that the greatest good comes from a much more integrated form of practice, in which architects, interior designers, engineers, landscape architects, and contractors work more closely together, makes this dispute over licensure seem like a battle from the last century. A more creative solution, and one that would allow both sides to transcend this self-defeating fight, might involve the licensing of the integrated teams that will increasingly create our built environment. We can become so intent on protecting our turf that we don't notice that the ground has shifted beneath us and that the turf we have so long protected may no longer matter.

Figure 26.2 Assemble, an interdisciplinary collaboration of architects, designers, and artists in the UK, show how disciplinary diversity can expand our thinking about the built environment, like this reuse of an abandoned petrol station as an outdoor theater.

Reference

Hohfeld, Wesley. 1978. *Fundamental Legal Conceptions*. Arthur Corbin (ed.). Westport, CN: Greenwood Press.

Chapter 27

Money laundering

An architect friend whose firm had designed a project in Dubai showed me a photo he took from a plane window as he landed in that city years ago, with a series of idiosyncratically capped towers popping out of the coastal fog like so many ornamental candles on a white-frosted cake. I asked him how that city came to have so many buildings constructed so quickly. He looked at me with a bit of surprise that I did not already know and then said two words: money laundering. Dubai has since done a lot to stem the tide of illicit funds into its banks and then into its buildings, but that hasn't stopped

Figure 27.1 The amount of dirty money in the global economy in need of laundering has greatly affected the building design and development industry, leading to more construction than markets may warrant, as in places such as Dubai.

money launderers from looking for other avenues to clean the dirty money that comes from the global drugs trade – much of which drives building development in some parts of the world.

Money laundering has long funded big projects around the world, although it remains little-discussed among architects. A quick perusal of the banking literature shows why buildings attract so much dirty money: you can buy them for cash and you can pay extraordinary amounts of money to upgrade them, again for cash, all of which can be explained as legitimate and entirely legal expenses. Real estate has been one of the fastest ways to launder money and many architects and developers have benefited from this, generating more demand for space than the marketplace might need. I asked my friend if it bothered him that some of the funds that paid for his project and his fees came from drug money and he said no. It was all part of doing business in Dubai back then, he said with a shrug. Ethics be damned.

Money laundering remains illegal in most places, however, and the more that architects look the other way, the more the profession becomes complicit in it, which itself represents a crime. In the US, the Money Laundering Control Act of 1986 (US Congress, 1986) makes it illegal to launder money from unlawful activities or to conceal the source, ownership, or control of those funds. The UK has gone even further in the Proceeds of Crime Act of 2002 (UK Parliament, 2002), which criminalizes concealing, failing to disclose, tipping off or just being involved with a money launderer, all which makes shrugging off such activity a possible path to prison or a sure way to suffer stiff penalties.

The fragmentation of the building and development industry, though, makes it hard to catch and easy to conceal such activity. Architects focus on designing and constructing buildings within the budgets a client gives them, rarely asking where the money came from or whether it was obtained legally or not, and yet many design professionals probably get a sense at some point in a project if a misalignment seems to exist between the funds being spent and what a particular client would likely have available. Large cash transactions for building products or professional services, for instance, should send a warning sign to architects, however much they may not want to acknowledge it, with what may otherwise be a very lucrative project. Ignoring such signs does not constitute a defense, since even indirect involvement in a money-laundered project creates culpability.

As in so many situations, it doesn't much matter what approach to ethics you consider; all lead to roughly the same conclusion. Virtue ethics would hold that looking the other way when suspecting the laundering of dirty money is imprudent and cowardly, while contract ethics would take the position that such behavior breaks the social contract of professionals by concealing criminal activity that society would want us to reveal. At the same time, duty ethics would have us blow the whistle on the money laundering simply because it is the right – and legally binding – thing to do, while utilitarianism would remind us of the greater good of the greatest number of people, which money laundering does little to advance.

Governments have made it easy to report money laundering. In the UK, the report would go to the National Crime Agency and in the US, the Department of the Treasury's Terrorism and Financial Intelligence unit. But governments themselves, or at least some powerful people in government, can become complicit in such laundering schemes. Donald Trump's development organization, for example, has licensed their name to buildings that have reportedly served as money laundries, from Panama to India to Indonesia (Blumenthals, 2017). The Trump Organization has also paid fines and settlements for money laundering, without ever admitting guilt, as if to shrug, much as my architect-friend did, and say that this is just how business gets done in the development field.

For legal as well as ethical reasons, the development industry needs to change this situation. The huge amounts of ill-gotten money flowing into real estate have led to over-development in some places, reflecting the amount of funds in need of laundering rather than what the market itself can sustain. That in turn can lead to structures that become albatrosses for communities, burdening them for years to come with overly ambitious and under-performing buildings. The use of dirty money to fund building projects also corrupts architecture, leading to the overly elaborate, highly complicated, and increasingly expensive designs that money launderers often

Figure 27.2 Some global financial institutions have become complicit in this dirty business, such as HSBC, which had to pay $1.9 billion (£1.4 billion) in fines in 2012 for helping Mexican drug cartels launder money.

want to wash as much cash as possible. That tends to reinforce the public opinion that some architects, at least, are not judicious in the use of clients' funds and work mainly for the super-rich, with little interest in, or time for, people or projects of more ordinary means. That may be unfair and, in most cases, untrue, but that bad rap remains a problem for the profession.

In that sense, drug money has become a drug to some in the development community, clouding professional judgment and encouraging architectural hallucinations. While the vast majority of architects and developers have stayed off this drug, its remains both highly alluring and widely available, depending on the place and the people involved in a project. Those who have succumbed to dirty money, knowingly or not, need treatment protocols, like any drug user. Ending the epidemic in drug use would reduce the amount of money in need of laundering, but until then, with so much cash continuing to circulate in the global development industry, the profession of architecture has but one option when asked to design a project built on dirty money: just say no.

References

Blumenthal, Paul. 2017. "Bribery, Corruption, Money Laundering: The Many Investigations into Trump Business Partners," *Huffington Post*, June 29. www. huffingtonpost.com/entry/trump-business-partners-investigations_us_59540f65e 4b05c37bb7bbbdb. Accessed May 21, 2018.

UK Parliament. 2002. *Proceeds of Crime Act, 2002, Chapter 29*. www.legislation. gov.uk/ukpga/2002/29/pdfs/ukpga_20020029_en.pdf. Accessed May 21, 2018.

US Congress. 1986. *Money Laundering Control Act of 1986*. www.ffiec.gov/bsa_aml_ infobase/documents/regulations/ml_control_1986.pdf. Accessed May 21, 2018.

Chapter 28

Moral foundations

Over my career, I have written about buildings situated in non-Western countries, and I have always felt torn in how to respond to architecture in such settings. How much do my Western values influence my response to their design, and how much do the people in these places embrace – or not – the Western ideas embodied in buildings designed by architects from Europe or North America? Also, how much do these structures represent an aspiration on the part of these clients to signal their connection to the global marketplace in which internationally known architects trade, or do they stand as foreign outposts of globalism in places that remained decidedly local and tradition-bound in character?

Such questioning led me to moral foundations theory, which seemed to provide, if not a simple answer, at least a way to think about global practice that I found helpful. Developed by the social psychologist Jonathan Haidt and his colleagues, Craig Joseph and Jesse Graham, this theory rests on an architectural analogy. As they note, they "chose the architectural metaphor of a 'foundation' . . . [because] the foundations are not the finished buildings, but the foundations constrain the kinds of buildings that can be built most easily . . . Similarly, the moral foundations are not the finished moralities, although they constrain the moral orders that can be built" (Haidt et al, 2013, p. 65).

These authors have identified five foundational ideas that they see as guiding people's judgments about right and wrong across many different cultures. They include:

1 The care and protection of others
2 Fairness and proportionality in how we interact with others
3 Loyalty to family, friends, group, and nation
4 Respect for authority and tradition
5 A sense of sanctity and avoidance of disgusting things
6 A love of liberty and freedom from coercion

Haidt and his colleagues then claim that Western, liberal democracies have greatly valued three of these foundational values – care, fairness, and liberty – while downplaying the other three – loyalty, authority, and sanctity – that many non-Western societies and more conservative citizens tend to value just as much. That argument has been controversial, especially in the West, since it suggests that liberalism has emphasized a narrower set of ethical values than conservatism, which these authors claim has tended to embrace all six foundational ideas more equally. We won't enter that debate. But moral foundations theory does offer a useful way of thinking about the relationship of architecture and ethics, particularly across Western and non-Western cultures.

Consider what, for many people, constitutes the most important building in their lives: their home. In many ways, the house, as a building type, epitomizes the foundational value of care, since it typically represents the place in which people share with their family members, seek solace in difficult times, and attend to the needs of some of the most important people in our lives. And while the details of those arrangements can differ greatly from one era and culture to another, home serves as the center of care.

But the varied forms that houses take over time and space also embrace equally diverse values. Modern designs, epitomized by Philip Johnson's iconic glass house, have embodied the foundational importance of liberty, with its "free plan" and near absence of interior walls. Johnson and his partner had a maximum of physical mobility, able to change the use of the internal space by simply rearranging furniture.

The limits of such liberty, though, come through in the idea that those who live in glass houses should not throw stones. We should not criticize others – not throw stones – when we are not willing to subject ourselves to the same criticism, an idea that lies at the heart of moral foundations theory: do not disparage others' values without first understanding how our values look to them. Johnson seemed to understand that, and built a nearly windowless structure near his glass house to which he and his partner could retreat after living with so little privacy within their glass walls. Those two structures express the paradox of liberty: the more we have, the more we yearn for, if not its opposite, at least some respite from it. To paraphrase Aristotle's ethics: too much of a good thing isn't a good thing.

The typical Western, single-family house emphasizes another foundational priority. Such houses take myriad forms, as varied as the clients they shelter and the communities and climates in which they stand, but most follow a basic formula of semi-private living, dining, and kitchen spaces into which guests can enter and stay, and more fully private bedrooms and bathrooms often located further from the front door. Unlike Johnson's house, these various functions – at least the most private ones – occupy separate rooms, of appropriate size to the role one has in the family.

As such, contemporary Western houses combine care with fairness and proportionality, where the relative size and relationship of rooms expresses the fair disposition and proportional arrangement of rights and

Figure 28.1 The primacy of "liberty" as a value in the West reached the pinnacle of architectural expression in Philip Johnson's Glass House, with its lack of interior walls and its glass enclosure creating a "free plan."

responsibilities of the home's occupants. Here, values trump functionality. A child might need more space than parents in a bedroom, given the time some youth spend in their rooms, but parents' frequently get the larger amount of square footage, tellingly called the master bedroom, because of the latter's greater position in the family. At the same time, children frequently get rooms roughly the same size, as a statement of the fairness that undergirds most Western families, regardless of whether one child might need more or less space than another.

Foundational values, even among Western countries, can vary widely from one culture to another. Although most houses in the UK or in Europe do not differ significantly from the gradation of more or less private spaces of the typical North American house, context does make a difference. Many more houses on the European continent, for instance, occupy existing buildings or share party walls with neighbors, often leading to a tighter configuration of rooms and a greater dialogue between old and new than found in North America. From an ethical perspective, that reflects a somewhat greater emphasis on tradition and authority – on respect for the past and existing urban fabric – than often found in more individualistic countries like the US or Canada.

However, as I have learned working with students from South Asia, authority, loyalty and sanctity remain much more dominant values in the housing there. In Kathmandu, Nepal, for example, the typical urban house is multi-level and multi-generational, with the older members of a family – parents, grandparents – on the lowest level and younger members of the family on upper floors, with living spaces and a rooftop terrace to take advantage of light and air, and with a prayer or meditation room located within the house itself. The accommodation of multiple generations of family members, with one generation watching over another, reflects the importance of loyalty to the extended family, while the inclusion of a space for prayer and meditation reveals the value placed on sanctity and on having a sacred space separate from the rest of the house and activities such as cooking or sanitation.

In parts of Kathmandu, a passage or *galli* connects the houses of several families on a block, enabling children or adults to move from one family courtyard to another without having to go out into the street. This creates a multi-household community that allows parents or grandparents to watch other children, whose own parents may be at work or on errands, and gives youth a degree of freedom to visit with friends or to have playmates without

Figure 28.2 Older Kathmandu houses have multiple generations living on different floors around a central courtyard connected to those of adjacent houses, reflecting the importance of values such as care, loyalty, sanctity, and respect for tradition.

having to depend on their parents for transportation or supervision. Such a setup shows how values such as care and freedom can take very different forms in different places. Care becomes the responsibility of many families for each other, and freedom exists under the watchful eye of friends and family, something quite different from the largely parental care and personal freedom embodied in the typical Western single-family house.

Such differences in how we dwell do not mean that one is better than another or that Western cultures do not care enough about loyalty and sanctity, or non-Western ones about freedom and fairness. All of the foundational values that Haidt and his colleagues have identified exist to different degrees in every community and in every family, or we wouldn't call them a community or a family. What this does mean, though, is that we need to listen carefully, especially when working in cultures different from our own, to what people value and prioritize in their lives and not just about what they need functionally or what the codes allow legally. The functionalism of modern architecture has its place, since no one wants to live or work in a dysfunctional building, but the reduction of architecture to function allowed some modernists to make the mistake of assuming that because all people have similar physical and biological needs as human beings, they also all share the same values, goals, and views of the world. The International Style, in that sense, represented a morally oppressive architecture, imposing not just an aesthetic, but also an ethics foreign to many people around the world. The glass, steel, and concrete towers that now exist in cities across the globe have sturdy enough physical foundations, but their moral foundations remain questionable and they stand, ethically, on shaky ground.

Reference

Haidt, Jonathan; Graham, Jesse; Koleva, Sena; Motyl, Matt; Iyer, Ravi; Wojcik, Sean; Ditto, Peter. 2013. "Moral Foundations Theory: The Pragmatic Validity of Moral Pluralism," *Advances in Experimental Social Psychology*, 47, 55–130.

Chapter 29

Moral hazard

We tend to associate hazards with physical perils, not ethical ones. But when people rig a system so that they cannot lose, regardless of how much they endanger others, it can present a moral hazard as dangerous as any material threat. And while we have done a lot to protect people from physical harm, the global economy has actually increased the presence of moral hazards and made it more likely that we will suffer from them as a result.

The evidence of this? In an era of growing inequality around the world, with 42 people now having the same amount of wealth as half of the remaining population, the rich seem to get richer no matter what happens to the economy, and the powerful seem to retain their power no matter how poorly they perform in office. Even the words "moral hazard" seem rigged. It carries the word "moral" even though it represents the height of immorality and fails by almost any measure of ethical behavior. Those who manipulate things so that they cannot lose seem cowardly, unjust, and imprudent; they violate any sense of the social contract; they use others as means to their ends; and they have figured out how to avoid the consequences of their own actions.

Yet moral hazard continues unabated in part because it hides in plain sight, easily mistaken as a form of insurance, even though it grossly distorts that valuable activity. Rather than reduce risk and protect policy holders from unanticipated adversity, as insurance has done so successfully for so many people, moral hazard protects a few at the expense of others, with the latter often not even aware of their exposure because of the irresponsible risks of a few, who feel free to gamble since others will pay the price of failure.

Architecture has suffered greatly from moral hazard and yet the field rarely acknowledges the presence of this practice. The global recession that began in 2008 stemmed from the moral hazard of banks, profiting from the lending of sub-prime mortgages to unwitting customers and then bundling those mortgages in ways that disguised their riskiness from those who bought them. The collapse of the global economy as a result of this risky behavior on the part of major banks affected all sectors and industries, and

Figure 29.1 Protests against the banks whose unwise lending led to the 2008 recession show the negative effect that morally hazardous behavior can have on the reputation of those who engage in it.

because it involved housing and the mortgage market, architects, contractors and developers took a greater hit than most.

This seems particularly ironic since architects have a duty as licensed professionals to protect the health, safety, and welfare of others, and as a result, the built environment has all sorts of over-sized and redundant features to ensure that buildings won't collapse, systems won't fail, and inhabitants won't get injured. Such protections against physical hazards aim to protect everyone. Moral hazards, though, flip the equation, protecting the few at the expense of the many, against which we have few safeguards. Those who engage in morally hazardous activity typically have knowledge not only of how systems work but also of who has the power to ensure that those systems will benefit them, with the general public often left holding the bag.

While many architects may take aesthetic risks, most have an aversion to the financial risks that typically define moral hazard. The opposite seems true in the financial community, which often has a very conservative aesthetic identity while taking sometimes reckless risks with others' money, having insulated themselves from the consequences of those decisions with government guarantees and taxpayer-funded bailouts. As the 2008 financial debacle showed, morally hazardous investment banking has become an economic hazard for everyone else.

The solution to moral hazard lies in ensuring that those who engage in unreasonable risk suffer the consequences of such behavior. On the policy level that means that governments should not bail out financial institutions that continue to engage in the kind of actions that led to the 2008 economic collapse. And that applies to individuals who take unreasonable risks as well. I heard from an architecture-school classmate about one of the members of our class who had gone to work on Wall Street instead of going into the profession. This architect-turned-financier had gotten into financial trouble because of risky investments and our classmate contacted us to see if we would loan him money to help bail him out of bankruptcy. Some said yes to this plea, but I refused, not because I lacked the funds but because of the moral hazard it represented: his taking undue risk and then expecting a financial rescue reminded me of the too-big-to-fail banks that expected the same during the recession. Moral hazard ends when people have to pay the price of their risky behavior and suffer the consequences of their choices. Those who live by the sword should be prepared to die by the sword, as the saying goes.

Figure 29.2 The structural sturdiness of the buildings along Wall Street belies the questionable ethics of what goes on inside, highlighting the contrast between a safe physical environment and a morally hazardous one.

Cases like his may seem obvious and easily addressed. Moral hazard, though, can slip into even the most routine activity, such as architectural contracts. An architect at a talk I gave about ethics complained, during the question and answer period, about contracts written by clients in such a way that they hold the architect liable even if not involved or responsible for a particular aspect of a project. A developer in the room responded to this comment before I could, asking: What is unethical about it? If architects willingly sign such contracts, then that is their decision and it has nothing to do with ethics, he argued.

The let-the-buyer-beware attitude of that developer assumes, of course, a level playing field among the parties involved in the contract and access to the same information, which rarely happens. Developers have the upper hand, able to keep shopping for architects until they find one who will sign their morally hazardous contract, while most architects have little ability to pick and choose their clients. But what such developers might gain in terms of getting more work for less money, they stand to lose in terms of their standing among others. And therein lies the irony of moral hazard. Once such behavior becomes known and others have borne the brunt of a no-win system or contract, people will shun those at fault. If there is a moral to the story of moral hazard, it is this: rigging a situation so as not to lose in the short run leads to losing, big time, in the long run.

Chapter 30

Nomadism

Architectural education accustoms us to think of the field's history beginning some 14,000 years ago, when the first permanent settlements began to appear, even though humans have made shelter for themselves since our start as a species, roughly 200,000 years ago. By dwelling on the last 5% of our past, the architectural discipline has largely ignored the other 93%, when nomadic communities moved frequently, deploying lightweight structures that they either carried with them or constructed on the spot and using the materials that they had at hand and that often biodegraded when no longer needed.

While the architecture curriculum still focuses on fixed-in-place structures and most people still live in permanent settlements, a small but growing number of people have begun to live more sparingly and to embrace a twenty-first-century version of the nomadic life. Seeking out portable, deployable, and demountable shelter and light, mobile, and responsive structures, these new nomads have embraced everything from tiny homes to micro-unit apartments to year-round camping. And academics have begun to study this increasingly mobile population, not just to help people find better accommodations, but also to learn from them, since they remain closer than most other groups to the nomadic existence that defined our ancestral past and that may increasingly characterize our future in the Anthropocene.

Technology has been a primary driver of this new nomadism. Mobile digital devices give us access to an amount of information and a level of capability far greater than other media have ever allowed, enabling us to access, download, and have delivered almost anything, anywhere, and at any time. Information can now go where buildings never could, which represents a remarkable disruption to architecture, as momentous as the advent of permanent structures fourteen millennia ago. Meanwhile, the architectural profession seems largely oblivious to this shift, even though the very idea of buildings as we know them has come into question.

That does not mean that we will all return to living a primitive life nor that people will no longer need buildings. We will always require shelter and enclosure, but in the future we may increasingly order our architecture online, having "buildings" delivered to us, and erected by us or others in

Figure 30.1 Tent designers have long raised questions about the nature of shelter, its relation to permanence, and how lightly we can live on the land – or in the air as these suspended tents in Belgium show.

much less time and for much less money that we now spend. Many architects may not want to make that shift or play in that world, but some will do so – and quite successfully, regardless of what the architectural schools and profession may think.

The sharing economy has become another driver of the new nomadism. A rapidly growing part of our economy, collaborative, peer-to-peer, and on-demand services offer new ways of living and working that represent a move away from the ownership and control of property and toward a model in which we pay for only what we use of other people's assets when available. This change in how we leverage resources and use space has altered how we think about real estate. Architecture has long depended on site control to accommodate its fixed structures and on clients to commission work on the land that that they own. Zoning regulations have reinforced that process by prohibiting uses and limiting heights and setbacks, ostensibly to preserve property values.

The new nomadism reflects the sharing-economy idea of owning as little as possible, renting the property of others when needed, and appropriating space as required. It also reflects larger transformations that may force this way of being upon most of us. Climate change, according to some estimates, will lead to millions of people becoming nomadic, fleeing coastal flooding, inland droughts, and extreme weather events to safer locations inland, near water sources. Economic disruptions will also propel this change. People stuck in places where jobs have disappeared will have to move to greater opportunities elsewhere, which in turn may prompt people to have fewer and lighter possessions to lessen what they have to transport. Our nomadic ancestors may have had little choice but to live this way, and our progeny may face the same thing.

Ethics arose, in part, to help our ancestors deal with the conflicts that arose from the claims of property; as John Locke wrote, "There can be no injury, where there is no property" (Locke, 1952). But unlike architecture, ethics has no fixed location; its ideas are as portable as the demountable buildings of nomads, and just as useful. The Native American code of ethics gives some sense of what nomadic people valued: prayer, gratitude, tolerance, hospitality, truthfulness, sharing, forgiveness, honoring others, respecting the earth (Nerburn, 1999). Such values reflected what people might need when living nomadically and requiring the assistance of others, and possibly encountering other tribes or communities of people in the process. It is an ethics of accommodation and a deeply spiritual and ecological one.

As people moved into permanent settlements, shelter became architecture and ethics became more codified. Some of the earliest ethical codes arose from Egypt, where the youth of the ruling class learned precepts about justice, humility, kindness, and respect of superiors, and from Babylon (now Iraq) where Hammurabi's Code took equity to an extreme in seeing justice

Figure 30.2 The annual "Burning Man" gathering in northwest Nevada now attracts over 65,000 people for a week of artistic and community activities in an instant city, laid out in an enormous semi-circle in the Black Rock Desert.

as taking an "eye for an eye, a tooth for a tooth" (Gordon, 1960). We can hear in such precepts the echo of an earlier nomadic ethics – humility, kindness, respect – as well as a new and somewhat more brutal one in Hammurabi's idea of absolute reciprocity.

These early efforts show how much ethics gave people living in permanent settlements needed guidance in how to relate and respond to each other, something that we still need today. While a nomadic existence had its stresses, so does a settled life, as we live near and work with the same unrelated people and interact constantly with strangers. As a result, we have ethics that echo those of ancient Egypt that focus on the development of our own character or virtue, as well as precepts, such as Hammurabi's, that are more action-oriented and based on duty and consequences.

But as we likely face a more nomadic future, one in which more people will move more often for the same reasons as our ancestors – for survival and for opportunity – we would do well to revisit both the architecture and the ethics of the earliest people. They knew how to carry a virtuous character with them as easily as their lightweight shelter and we may need to relearn that lesson as we live through the age of the Anthropocene, having affected the natural world as never before and having responsibility for it in ways that ancient nomadic people would have understood.

References

Gordon, Cyrus. 1960. *Hammurabi's Code*. New York: Holt, Rinehart and Winston.
Locke, John. 1952. *Concerning Civil Government*. Chicago: University of Chicago Press, Vol. 35.
Nerburn, Kent. 1999. *The Wisdom of the Native Americans*. Novato, CA: New World Library.

Chapter 31

Politics

Ethics and politics once had a close relationship, with the former offering guidance to the latter, but as politics has become more extreme, it has also become more distant from ethics. An example of this happened when an architect from a wealthy suburb got elected to the state legislature as a Republican, eventually letting his architectural license lapse as he rose in the ranks of conservative politics. His professional colleagues wondered what he would do when in office: would he vote for issues such as mass transit and walkable communities that matter most to architects or would he vote with his political party, generally opposed to such ideas? And why, I wondered, were matters pertaining to a better built environment a political issue at all? Why wouldn't some on the political right want healthier, safer communities just as much as someone on the political left?

A hyper-political relative of mine brought these questions to the fore when he assumed that, as a professor, I taught my students a left-wing ideology. What, I asked, is left- or right-wing architecture? Is a modern building left-wing and a classical one right-wing? And if that is the case, why do so many conservative groups have their headquarters in modern office buildings? Those questions led him to change the subject, but it left me wondering about the relationship of architecture to politics and the ethics behind that connection.

On its face, the design of buildings, landscapes, and communities remains an apolitical activity, since all people, liberal and conservative, need shelter – places in which to live, work, shop, study, and play. It should not matter where one stands on a range of other political issues, since everyone has a right to shelter, although even there, in dealing with the homeless who lack a place to sleep, some have turned that issue into a political one, as if helping the homeless somehow coddles their behavior or weakens their moral fiber. At one level, architecture stands as a technical field, a STEM field, more involved in keeping the rain out than in worrying about which political party reigns.

At another level, though, because the construction industry involves large investments, both public and private, it invariably gets entangled in politics.

Figure 31.1 The built environment rarely expresses ethical ideas as directly as this Dublin building does, urging us to have courage in the face of the political instability and economic uncertainty that often besets us.

Politicians make decisions that directly affect the amount of construction that occurs, either through appropriations of public money or through monetary and tax policies that influence private investments in buildings. And the construction industry, like all major sectors of the economy, has lobbyists who try to sway the opinions of politicians, left and right, about issues of concern.

Politics, though, remains as fluid a field as design and in recent decades, the political spectrum has become more like a barbell, with two opposing sides and almost no one in the middle. Many analysts have tried to explain this political polarization, attributing it to everything from radio talk shows and factional media to the growing disparity between a super-rich minority and everyone else. Whatever the cause, however, the implications for architects have become clear.

Architects, as individuals, no doubt have a wide range of political opinions. But architecture, as a discipline, does have commitments to improving the quality of life and enhancing the public realm. And that, at least in our current climate, seems to place the field, politically, toward one end of the barbell and not the other. Modern politics has become not a matter of negotiation over how different political parties will achieve common goals, but instead a matter of arguing whether common goals even exist.

It reminds me of Aristotle's ethical maxim that the good lies in the median between two extremes, where political parties have wandered to the extremes, especially Republicans to the extreme right, and forgotten their ethical responsibility to find the middle ground between those political poles (Aristotle, 1952). Architects rarely have the luxury of extremism. To get a building built requires all kinds of negotiation, which works against taking extreme positions of any kind. But politics doesn't always obey the same rules; many elected officials seem goaded on by their most vocal and involved constituents, who tend to have the most polarizing points of view.

One such polarity revolves around whether the public sector is part of the solution to problems or the problem itself. In the past, the political left and right would debate how best to finance public education, public healthcare, public transportation, and the like, but now the debate sometimes becomes more about whether or not we should have an adequately funded public realm or an adequately staffed public sector at all. Such anti-government sentiments have, as a consequence, led some to want to "privatize" a lot of what people formerly assumed to be the government's role, with public funds providing vouchers for people to go to private schools, with public healthcare viewed as a government takeover of the private market, and with public transportation seen as an unnecessary expenditure that benefits only a few.

Figure 31.2 Right- and left-wing politicians might argue over the funding of public space, but we are social animals, as Aristotle said, and most ourselves when occupying public spaces like this one in Bamberg, Germany.

Architects, of course, work for both public and private clients and so benefit regardless of whether public or private investments prevail. But the discipline's long tradition of advocacy for the public realm does place the field at odds with political conservatives and does suggest that architects have a duty to oppose extreme efforts to privatize everything we once thought of as public. Just as doctors advocate for health, and lawyers for justice, architects need to advocate for that which improves people's lives, their physical surroundings, and the public realm generally.

Some, like that architect-turned-legislator, may not agree. He faces the pressures of his party to vote according to their wishes, which may or may not reflect his ideas or values. This in turn raises the question: does our ethical duty as professionals trump our political ideology as individuals? The answer to that may depend upon how ideological the person or how dutiful the professional might be, but the ethics here seems clear and not equivocal. Professionals have an obligation to speak out for what research and experience have shown to be right, however unpopular that might be to political ideologues, who seem to have the answer to everything before the questions even get asked. And more professionals should consider following in the footsteps of that legislator-architect, not to become political ideologues, but to show how design can overcome polarization by getting people of all political stripes in communities to work on common problems and shared projects. It's the ethical thing to do.

Reference

Aristotle. 1952. *Nicomachean Ethics*. Chicago: University of Chicago Press, Vol. 9.

Chapter 32

Power

A graduate student whose thesis I supervised many years ago wrote to me recently, telling me about how another professor had harassed her when she took his courses, and expressing the fear that this caused her at the time and the anger that she still feels about it. She explained how this professor initially liked her work and then turned against her and gave her low grades for reasons she didn't know, suggesting that she meet with him in his office one-on-one for special tutoring. Faculty members, of course, meet in their offices with students all the time, but the way he framed this with her made her feel uncomfortable. Why her and not the other students? Why in his office rather than in the studio space, with other students around? Did he want to help her or did he have ulterior motives that she interpreted as harassment? She felt caught between not wanting to accede to his advances and her not wanting to get a bad grade in his class.

I told her how much I empathized with her because of the harassment I had encountered while a graduate student by a male researcher much older than me, who because I did not have a girlfriend at the time, assumed that I was gay. And because I was his research assistant, working on a funded project with him, we had more of an employer-employee relationship than a professor-student one, which I learned provides even more opportunity for predatory behavior because of one-on-one meetings without others around. This story may have surprised my former graduate student, since harassment, often by men, frequently has women as its target, but not always. Predators seem to care little about who constitutes their prey.

Nietzsche recognized this with his skepticism about ethics. For him, morals served as a disguise, a kind of mask as he put it, for the real motive of people's behavior: power over others. I've long thought that universities wear that mask, with their high-flown and oft-stated ideals about the value of education occurring within an institutional setting that, like the Catholic Church, creates power dynamics that favor those in control – professors, priests – and that silence those without it – students and, to a degree, staff. Of course, the vast majority of people in positions of power do not abuse that privilege and treat others with all the respect and honor that they

Figure 32.1 Confession booths in the Catholic Church have historically had elaborate architectural treatment as small buildings, an expression of the power differences that exist between priests and parishioners.

deserve as fellow human beings. Nietzsche's nihilism serves more as a warning than anything else, reminding us of the will-to-power that drives some people and of the need to put checks in place so that the people who seek power for their own ends do not have power or cannot use it against others if they do.

This has particular relevance for architecture. Because of the difficulty and expense of creating buildings, the field often finds itself having to accommodate the whims of powerful people, reinforcing the privileges of those who have the money to commission architects. Again, most clients do not abuse that power. They listen to reason, respect the expertise of professionals, care about others affected by their project, and pay their consultants and contractors for services rendered. But some do not, such as the developer Donald Trump. He became notorious in the development industry for rarely listening to, respecting, or paying his architects, and using his lawyers to threaten those who challenged his right to do what he wanted.

Abuse can come not just from clients, but also in architectural offices and schools. The sexual harassment charges of employees against a noted architect shows how much the power differential in firms can lead those in charge to abuse their staff – until, of course, they get called out and their reputation is ruined. I saw similar sexual harassment of female students by faculty during my time in architecture school, with one fellow student, years later, still scarred by the experience, despite her having become a successful architect in her own right. As I learned from my own harassment, people can overcome such encounters, but we should not have to do so in the first place. The "Me Too" movement, in calling out sexual predators wherever they are regardless of their power or prestige, deserves everyone's support, men as much as women.

The ethical issue here seems clear: the powerful have a responsibility to use that power wisely and not abuse those who lack it. Indeed, a recurring theme in the history of ethics has to do with protecting the powerless in the face of those who would take advantage of them. But what power does ethics have in altering predatory behavior? It offers us a timepiece, ticking away until that behavior blows up their careers and their lives. That may not seem like a persuasive deterrent to predators, whose desires appear to overwhelm their judgment, but it does offer a degree of consolation in knowing that unethical actions eventually catch up with those who engage in them.

That timepiece does not tick as fast as most of us might want. Trump becoming a US President shows how little some voters seem to care about his unethical behavior and it suggests that the consequences of his behavior may have a longer time horizon than those who care about ethics might want to admit. While Trump has seemingly prospered despite his unethical practices, appearances can be deceiving. His lack of ethics as a developer had already caught up with him by the time he ran for president, since most banks would no longer loan him money and most people in the design and construction industry refused to work for him, leading his company to became a franchiser of his name on buildings that others developed. As of this writing, Trump's unethical behavior has yet to overtake his presidency, but the clock keeps ticking and that will eventually happen, whether it be during his administration or in what historians say about it afterward.

Ethics, in other words, involves a temporal dimension: looking ahead and anticipating the impact of actions and decisions made today, something that architects, designers and planners do all the time when envisioning possible future environments for clients and communities. It also involves looking back, as my student did in writing about her interactions with that studio professor years before. Nietzsche had a pessimistic view of progress, with a cyclical view of time – an "eternal return" – in which the same issues recur again and again in human history (Nietzsche, 1974). That may be true at the broadest temporal scale, but in the timeframe of a person, as my student showed, ethics can help us make progress. What she experienced two decades ago, which she reported to authorities at the time, changed policies and procedures at the University and made the behavior of that professor

Figure 32.2 Chicago's Trump Tower, with its finger-like tower, makes what looks like a vulgar gesture to the city, which seems fitting for a developer-turned-politician who speaks of cities in mostly negative terms.

unacceptable and a cause for termination. Ethics may seem powerless in the face of powerful people, but it has a temporal power that those who lack a sense of ethics are powerless against.

Reference

Nietzsche, Friedrich. 1974. *The Gay Science.* New York: Random House.

Chapter 33

Practice

Charles Dickens, who wrote so perceptively about capitalism's human toll, captured the inequities of the architectural profession in his caricature of the lazy, greedy architect Seth Pecksniff in the novel *Martin Chuzzlewit* (Dickens, 2016). Chuzzlewit and his co-worker Tom Pinch work for Pecksniff, who presents their work as his own and who, instead of paying them, charges them tuition in exchange for teaching them about architecture. While Pecksniff's exploitative behavior sounds extreme, it foreshadowed that of Frank Lloyd Wright, who, during the Great Depression, turned his office into a "school" and started to charge his staff tuition, off which he – like Pecksniff – lived.

In his deeply ethical novels, Dickens showed how people readily take advantage of others for their own profit and how, as happens with Pecksniff in the end, it leads to their ruin. With Frank Lloyd Wright, though, it had the opposite effect. He remains honored as "the greatest architect of the 19th century" as Philip Johnson wryly described him, and his school remains open, although now divorced from the architectural firm, which has ceased operation (Saffron, 2016). Ruin, in architecture, may take longer, but for the unscrupulous, as Dickens observed, it eventually comes.

The conflict of interest in the profession between work and education affects far more than the few students-as-staff-members in Frank Lloyd Wright's firm. Many architectural schools, for example, have practitioners teaching in the design studios, a tradition that dates back to nineteenth-century architectural education in France's Ecole des Beaux Arts, where students often worked on projects that the faculty member had in the office. Students can learn a lot when working on such "real" projects and getting feedback from the faculty members working on the same projects themselves. But this creates a number of ethical problems. It exploits students whose ideas, like those of Chuzzlewit and Pinch, may get used without credit; it gives teaching practitioners an unfair advantage over their competitors; and it constitutes unpaid labor, which is illegal in many countries.

In 1994, I wrote an article for *Progressive Architecture*, entitled "The Intern Trap," that focused on the problem of well-known firms either not

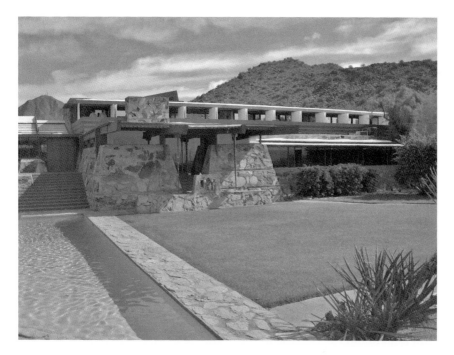

Figure 33.1 Frank Lloyd Wright not only had his staff pay him as his "students," starting in the Great Depression, but he also had them do physical labor, such as the construction of Wright's winter home and office, Taliesin West.

paying their interns or using sleights-of-hand, such as calling their interns "consultants," to avoid paying health benefits or withholding taxes. The American Institute of Architects responded with policies that strongly discouraged members and firms from engaging in such activities, and those policies – plus the very real criminal penalties that come with violations of labor or tax laws – seem to have greatly reduced the incidence of such behavior.

That does not mean that architectural interns have no more challenges. Some interns remain underutilized, with limited exposure to many aspects of architecture practice; poorly paid, often at the bottom of the firm's pay scale; and pigeonholed in firms as the "CAD jockey." But this situation has also begun to change. Practices that treat their interns well now get recognized with awards, such as the "Firm of the Year" award by the AIA, and competitive pressures on offices to attract and keep talented staff have led to much better conditions for interns.

The problems that interns face are precisely the ones the profession faces as a whole. The firm that does not adequately value its interns also devalues itself; the office that does not mentor interns can expect little collegiality in return; the employers who underpay an intern often accept inadequate compensation themselves; and the architects who exploit their own open the door to exploitation by others. In other words, how the youngest members of the profession get treated determines how clients and communities, consultants and contractors will treat us, and if we hope to change the conditions of architecture practice, it must begin with the most vulnerable among us: interns.

Nor is this an issue only in architectural firms. As Derek Thompson writes in *The Atlantic*, "Estimates put the number of unpaid interns every year between 500,000 and one million. So, in a country where working for free is mostly illegal, a student population somewhere between the size of Tucson and Dallas will be working for free, in plain view" (Thompson, 2012). Thompson solicited comments about unpaid internships and the many responses he received in defense of this practice shows the prevalence of what in ethics is called the "self-serving bias," in which people remain blind to how much self-interest affects their own actions, even when they see such self-serving actions in others. A related phenomenon is the paradox of abusive behavior, in which people abused as youths have a greater tendency to become abusive themselves when older. While I know of no evidence of this behavior among architects, I once had a conversation with an elderly practitioner who saw nothing wrong with unpaid interns because he went unpaid as an intern himself.

Figure 33.2 The history of long hours and underpayment for the amount of time worked goes back at least 100 years, in habits picked up during architecture schools, as the students in this 1919 photo suggest.

The exploitation of young workers also assumes that there is a plethora of talented employees willing to submit to such treatment, when in fact, the opposite is true. Workforce shortages have become a major issue in the construction industry for years and skilled employees – not employers – have the upper hand and they will avoid firms that do not treat their staff well. Likewise, firms with poor personnel practices create disgruntled employees who can have a direct effect on the bottom line, hampering the firm's performance, lowering its profitability, and reducing the service it provides. The recession that began in 2008 led many recent graduates – as well as older staff members who found themselves unemployed – to seek new careers that offered more money, more stability, or both, with few of them returning to architectural practice once the economy turned around. At the same time, many guidance counselors in schools came to see architecture as a field to avoid and advised their students accordingly, leading to a decrease in enrollments that has left many firms now unable to find enough staff to meet current demands.

This has created a situation that Dickens would have appreciated. Rather than being a field full of Pecksniff's, exploiting staff for profit and glory, architecture has become a field of Chuzzlewits, with young people seeking opportunities wherever they can and keeping their wits about them in the volatile conditions that capitalism creates for architects. And architects need to become more "Chuzzlewit" themselves, since the world has plenty of Pecksniff clients ready to take advantage whenever possible of practitioners who undervalue their expertise and under-sell their services. As Dickens wrote in the novel, "No man can expect his children to respect what he degrades" (Dickens, 2016, p. 527).

References

Dickens, Charles. 2016. *Life and Adventures of Martin Chuzzlewit*. The Project Gutenberg EBook #968.

Saffron, Inga. 2016. "In 'Architecture's Odd Couple' It's Philip Johnson vs. Frank Lloyd Wright," *New York Times*. July 1. www.nytimes.com/2016/07/03/books/review/architectures-odd-couple-philip-johnson-and-frank-lloyd-wright.html. Accessed May 21, 2018.

Thompson, Derek. 2012. "Work is Work: Why Free Internships are Immoral." *The Atlantic*. May 14, 2012. www.theatlantic.com/business/archive/2012/05/work-is-work-why-free-internships-are-immoral/257130/. Accessed May 21, 2018.

Chapter 34

Preservation

I graduated from college into the teeth of a recession and the only job I could find in my field was with the government, which had funded architectural preservation at a substantial level in preparation for the US bicentennial. I worked in preservation for several years, believing in its ethic of reusing resources rather than the widespread demolition that came under that Orwellian term: urban renewal. I continually confronted the conflict in a culture that spared no expense to preserve the life of a person and that spent so little to preserve the life of a building.

In an article on the ethics of abortion, the philosopher Don Marquis argued that we don't allow murder because it causes its victims to lose all of the "activities, projects, experiences, and enjoyments" that they would have had. "What makes killing any adult human being prima facie seriously wrong is the loss of his or her future," wrote Marquis (Marquis, 1989, p. 189–190). We can extend that same argument to the premature ending of the life of a perfectly good building. While the word "life" has a different meaning when we apply it to a living being as opposed to an inanimate object like a building, the ethics related to terminating a life appear as relevant to buildings as much as bodies. Demolishing something that still has a promising future raises the same kind of objections we have when we see someone negligently or intentionally killing someone else. It deprives people of the "activities, projects, experiences, and enjoyments" that they might have had in that building.

Drawing a parallel between killing a person and demolishing a building may seem extreme. Buildings have no political rights, no feeling of pain, no interpersonal relationships or any of the other characteristics of a human life that make murder so immoral. Nor, since the abolition of slavery, do we allow one person to own another, the way we do buildings. The private-property rights that accrue to the owner of a building gives that person relatively free reign to tear it down, except in those few instances where historic designations or other contractual agreements prohibit it.

Law and ethics, though, almost never perfectly align. What the law allows us to do does not necessarily make it ethical, which Marquis's

PENN.R.R.STATION FROM GIMBEL SHOP, NEW YORK

Figure 34.1 The demolition of Pennsylvania Station in New York City galvanized the preservation community and its loss deprived millions of people of the experiences and enjoyments of that building.

argument highlights. We can legally engage in war, for example, but that does not make the killing of other people ethical because, as Marquis observes, it deprives them of their future, which we have no right to take. At the same time, Marquis argues for the ethics of mercy killing, of ending the life of a terminally ill person who wants to die because of the pain and suffering that their foreshortened future holds for them, even though this remains illegal, at least in the US.

This gives us criteria of when to save a building and when not to. If a structure still has "life" in it, with enough structural integrity and physical capacity to accommodate a variety of new uses, we should do all we can to preserve and rehabilitate it. And if not – if its deterioration has so shortened its life and made its reuse almost impossible without a nearly complete rebuilding – we should not hesitate demolishing it unless there is some extraordinary value attached to the structure to merit its reconstruction.

That, then, raises the question of value to whom? What may have little or no value to one person might mean everything to another. Take the case of the Ise Jingu shrine in Japan, which gets rebuilt every two decades and that, by some accounts, has been in that location in that same form for some 2000 years (Nuwer, 2013); it clearly has had value to a community of worshipers for a very long time, who demolish it only to reconstruct it exactly as it was. In that sense, the death of a building becomes ritualized, as we do with the death of a person, through various burial practices meant to memorialize the life of a person who has passed. The Ise Jingu remains a rarity in this regard, since the passing of buildings hardly ever gets memorialized in the way we do a person, even though their loss can have as much of an emotional effect on us as the loss of other people and in some cases, even more so, since we don't inhabit another person as we do the buildings we might call home.

Marquis's deprivation argument, that we don't have the right to deprive others of a future like our own, has been used by those who oppose abortion, but does it have equal bearing on the end of life, be that of a person or a piece of property? At first glance, no, since those at the end of life have little future we can deprive them of. And yet a piece of architecture, unlike a person, can last forever if we choose to spend the money and effort to preserve it. Buildings, in other words, always have a future, which, according to Marquis's argument, gives us no ethical ground to demolish them, despite our legal right to do so.

Figure 34.2 The Ise Jingu shrine has been continuously rebuilt, showing the difference between the finite length of a human life and the potentially infinite length of the life of a building, if we care to preserve it.

I eventually left the preservation field, discouraged by the often-rigid opposition that some preservationists took toward anything modern, living far too much in the past for my taste. But I also tired of what felt like a losing battle against the commercial culture of the US that often saw buildings only in terms of their resale value rather than anything inherent in their design, their history, or their reuse potential. The preservation field, though, has never left me. After growing up in an era in which the future seemed to care little about the past, the coming years seem poised to reverse that course. In the past, the future somehow became synonymous with futurism and its fascination with speed and technology, but the need for us to live more resiliently in the future will demand that we look to the past, when most people lived that way, for clues in how to do this. There is, in other words, a real future for the past, if we hope to have any future at all.

References

Marquis, Don. 1989. "Why Abortion is Immoral". *Journal of Philosophy* LXXXVI, 4, April, 183–202.

Nuwer, Rachel. 2013. "This Japanese Shrine has been Torn Down and Rebuilt every 20 years of the Past Millennium," *Smithsonian*. October 4. www.smithsonianmag. com/smart-news/this-japanese-shrine-has-been-torn-down-and-rebuilt-every-20-years-for-the-past-millennium-575558/. Accessed May 21, 2018.

Chapter 35

Privacy

I think of myself as a very private person, although I don't know what that means anymore. If anything, I think many people will look back on the last 100 years as a period in which the idea of privacy became especially problematic. Privacy once distinguished architecture from most of the other arts: architects traditionally created private and semi-private rooms in buildings that defined the levels of intimacy among the people who inhabited them. Most buildings, of course, still do so, just as most have a public presence like other visual and performing arts, but architecture's historic role of providing privacy began to change in the early twentieth century.

When Mies van der Rohe envisioned his early glass-clad towers, they challenged not only people's aesthetic sensibilities, but also their assumption that architecture would provide them with privacy. Living and working in glass-walled spaces, with few walls between different types of activities, represented a profound turn in architecture's purpose and reflected an equally tectonic shift in Western culture. Personal freedom seemed to become more important than a person's privacy, evident in the "free plans" that architecture increasingly offered.

Many people also started to use the growing physical freedom that some twentieth-century technology allowed to pursue more privacy. The suburban sprawl that arose around many cities, particularly after World War II, epitomized that trend, as people sought more privacy on larger plots of land even as they installed more picture windows and inhabited more open interior spaces that provided less privacy. The latter may have prompted the former: increased space between buildings partially compensated for the greater visual exposure within and immediately around them, but this shows the ambivalence that many people had about privacy, wanting more of it as they had less of it.

Ethics reflected this as much as architecture. The lawyer and feminist scholar Catharine MacKinnon has highlighted the oppressive role that privacy can play in shielding the abuse of women and children on the part of men in the home, while others, such as the lawyer and philosopher Anita Allen, have pointed out that the loss of privacy also makes everyone vulnerable to

Figure 35.1 Mies van der Rohe's Farnsworth House epitomizes the shift from privacy to personal freedom in the twentieth century, even though Dr. Edith Farnsworth found little freedom in the house's lack of privacy.

the surveillance of others, be it prying neighbors or an intrusive government (MacKinnon, 1989; Allen, 1988). Both sides of this debate have merit and it has led to an emerging consensus that privacy has value up to a point and that everyone should have the right to find their own balance between privacy and visibility in their lives.

This has its architectural equivalent in the open and flowing interiors and the shaded and screened exteriors of so many buildings in recent years, expressing the flexibility and informality that has come to characterize private life, at least in Western countries, while also reflecting the growing density and intensity of the public sphere. That re-balancing also seems underway at the urban scale. While suburban sprawl continues in some places, an increasing number of existing suburbs have tried to become more urban as they seek higher densities, more walkable neighborhoods, and a bigger tax base. At the same time, people have begun to flock to cities worldwide as part of the rapid urbanization of the human population, suggesting that, while privacy still matters, so does community and proximity.

The very word "privacy" prompts these varied interpretations. It shares with words such as privation and privilege the same Latin root word – privatus – which means personal, peculiar, separate, and deprived, meanings that have both positive and negative connotations. Privacy can seem like a privilege and something to seek, and a privation and something to avoid. And those opposite connotations perhaps explain our cycling back and forth over the last century, as some people still pursue privacy in suburban locations and others re-populate cities, away from the privation of remote living.

This sense of privacy as both privilege and privation has affected the digital world as much as the physical one. Social media and electronic mail have made communications among people distantly located much faster and easier, which has enhanced the productivity of workers and the speed with which work gets done. These digital tools, though, also entice some people to reveal more about themselves and their opinions than might be wise. Electronic communications now make it too easy for someone to send a private and intemperate message to a large number of people, any of whom can forward it on to others not meant to see it.

Like privacy, the virtue of temperance has acquired a negative connotation, evoking the Temperance Movement's call for abstinence from alcohol.

Figure 35.2 Louis Kahn's Yale Center for British Art show a degree of temperance in its use of materials and self-control in its details that provides a model of how we all might behave in an intemperate and un-self-controlled modern world.

Temperance, however, originally meant restraint, control, and most importantly, self-control: the temperate person knew when to speak and when to keep quiet, when to act and when to stand back, and when to reveal something and when not to. Balancing the freedom that social media provides with the temperance that some of its users so desperately need parallels the need to weigh personal freedom against privacy. In both cases, what technology allows us to do can overwhelm our capacity for self-control and our appreciation of restraint.

Architecture might remind us of such values. Buildings, long the bulwark of privacy, can quickly reveal the consequences of a lack of self-control, be it glass walls that require constant covering or open plans that demand later partitions. The laws of physics and the norms of society require that architecture exists within limits and that it not reveal too much, lest it cease to serve our needs. Architecture uses technology – and deploys plenty of digital technology – in its design, construction, and operation, and the functional role it plays in our lives forces us to draw a line between visibility and privacy, revelation and restraint.

In this, architecture can seem old-fashioned, especially in an era in which some of what we once did in buildings – such as learn, shop, and read – can now happen anywhere, indoors or out. But as some of the old functions of buildings have transferred to the digital environment, we will likely discover new reasons for architecture's being, not just in the provision of structures that keep us warm and dry – a purpose that will never go away – but also as places in which we learn the value of privacy and the merits of tempering our natural – and often self-defeating – desire to live without constraint.

References

Allen, Anita. 1988. *Uneasy Access: Privacy for Women in a Free Society.* Totowa, NJ: Rowman & Littlefield.
MacKinnon, Catharine. 1989. *Toward a Feminist Theory of the State.* Cambridge: Harvard University Press.

Chapter 36

Productivity

The older I get, the more obsolete I seem to become. While I keep up with the controversies of my field and key issues in my discipline, I find myself forever falling behind on the tools my students use as they have moved from computer visualization to virtual reality and augmented reality. I still largely draw by hand, taking comfort in the comment Marshall McLuhan once made that new technology tends to turn the old technology into an art form. I am certainly no artist with it comes to hand drawing, but I have come to accept the fact that I will never be as productive as my students and younger colleagues, regardless of how fast I apply pen to paper.

But increased productivity is no longer the benefit it once was. According to the Economic Policy Institute, worker productivity between 1948 and 1973 in the US increased 96.7% and pay kept up with it, increasing 91.3%.

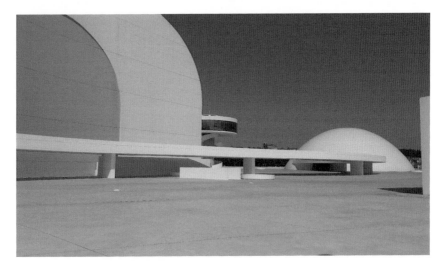

Figure 36.1 The Brazilian architect, Oscar Niemeyer, worked until nearly 105, with projects such as the Centro Niemeyer underway in his last years, showing just how productive an aging workforce can be.

But between 1973 and 2016, productivity increased 73.7% and wages only 12.3% (EPI, 2017). While the US Bureau of Labor statistics shows that this gap narrows somewhat if pay gets measured against the value of the goods and services produced, the fact remains that salaries have not kept pace with productivity, except at the very top of organizations, where executive pay has often soared (Brill et al, 2017). Nor is this just a US phenomenon. As the International Labour Organization has shown, this gap exists across industrial economies globally, with average industrial productivity growing more than twice as much as average wages between 1999 and 2011 (Renner, 2013).

Architects have experienced this firsthand. Between the increasing power and capacity of digital design tools and the growing speed with which information can get shared and worked on almost anywhere around the globe, the productivity of architectural offices has grown enormously. But wages have grown only modestly, not exceeding 3% between 2012 and 2018, which suggests that the beneficiaries of the increased productivity among architects have been clients, able to get more from firms, faster, better, and cheaper than before (Hanley Wood Data Studio, 2018).

Why that increased productivity has not translated into much higher wages remains a question. Many explanations exist for that stagnation of wages overall, from increasing global competition that has suppressed wages in the most developed countries to public policies that have mostly benefited the people with the most money to give to politicians: the top wage earners. But architecture seems to have its own challenges. In part because of the productivity gains, small firms with low overhead can now compete with much larger offices, depressing the fees of all. And increased productivity has not always translated into faster production, but instead into more time for design, which can lead to better results, or not.

The aging of the profession may also factor in here. In the US, over 35% of architects are over the age of 55 (Baker, 2018), and similar statistics hold in Europe, where one third of the profession is under 40 and two-thirds over (Mirza & Nacey, 2015, p. 1–16). History has shown that older people caught in a technological or economic transition, trained in a previous era without new skills, often face higher unemployment. That happened with in the nineteenth-century industrial revolution and it appears to be happening again with the digital revolution. But while economics may work that way, leaving older workers behind, ethics and politics do not, and the latter have a responsibility to help people transition to new economic and technical realities.

Ignoring that obligation can create havoc in countries. The number of people angered by feeling left behind in the global economy had an impact on the Brexit vote in the UK and on Donald Trump's election in the US, both of which reflected a desire by some in those countries for more nationalistic and protectionist policies as a buffer against the rapid change brought by the global, digitally-based economy. And if the political reasons for not leaving older workers behind are not clear enough, the ethical reasons should be. We help others in need, especially the older members of a society, because we, too, will age and find ourselves in need of help someday. Treat others as we will want to be treated.

The challenge economically lies in the mismatch between the productivity and pay of older workers, at the peak of their earning power while less productive than colleagues half their age. But what we mean by productivity may need questioning. While older practitioners may not be as productive on the computer as younger members of the profession, the former are likely far more productive when it comes to the things that only experience can provide. Malcolm Gladwell's argument that proficiency comes only after 10,000 hours – or 5 years of full-time work – rings true here, with older workers able to make some decisions more quickly and to respond to some situations more confidently (Gladwell, 2008). Which suggests that productivity can take many forms, some of it having to do with the tools we use and some of it, from the life we have lived.

A healthy labor force, in other words, needs to embrace both younger and older workers. An ethically grounded one, however, needs to question

Figure 36.2 Christ Lutheran Church in Minneapolis was one of the last completed buildings of Eliel Saarinen and its addition, one of the last completed buildings of his son, Eero. They both worked until the very end of their lives.

the pay disparities that exist between the two groups: why do older workers, who may no longer have the kinds of expenses that younger people in the midst of raising families or paying tuition, have much higher salaries? What if pay followed a bell curve over time, with the youngest and oldest workers making less than those in middle age, at the height of financial need? Higher education offers one model here. The emeritus title given to older faculty allow them to continue to work at a much lower pay and at a pace that each individual finds most comfortable. The same occurs in some professional offices when partners sell their ownership of a firm and work at reduced hours or on only select projects.

What if that system existed across the economy? Rather than have an increasing pay scale until retirement, at which point senior people leave an organization entirely, there existed a path in which older employees tapered off their involvement while mentoring younger staff, advising on difficult business decisions, and providing institutional memory and historical insights that only experience can give. Call this "productive retirement," in which older people would feel valued for what they have learned and not feel put out to pasture and forgotten, as happens too often in today's work world. Emeritus employees would cost an organization little, while adding a lot to the efficacy of its operations; extending what professors and other professionals now enjoy to the entire workforce seems like a simple way to improve everyone's productivity.

References

Baker, Kermit. 2018. "How Many Architects Does our Economy Need?" *Architect*. January 5. www.architectmagazine.com/aia-architect/aiafeature/how-many-architects-does-our-economy-need_o. Accessed May 21, 2018.

Brill, Michael; Holman, Corey; Morris, Chris; Raichoudhary, Ronjoy; Yosif, Noah. 2017. "Understanding the Labor Productivity and Compensation Gap," *Beyond the Numbers* [Bureau of Labor Statistics], 6(6). www.bls.gov/opub/btn/volume-6/pdf/understanding-the-labor-productivity-and-compensation-gap.pdf. Accessed May 21, 2018.

Economic Policy Institute. 2017. *The Productivity-Pay Gap*. October. www.epi.org/productivity-pay-gap/. Accessed May 21, 2018.

Gladwell, Malcolm. 2008. *Outliers: The Story of Success*. New York: Little Brown.

Hanley Wood Data Studio. 2018. "BLS: 148,000 Jobs Added in December," *Architect*. Jan 05. www.architectmagazine.com/practice/bls-148-000-jobs-added-in-december_o. Accessed May 21, 2018.

Mirza & Nacey Research. 2015. *The Architectural Profession in Europe, 2014: A Sector Study*. Brussels: Architects' Council of Europe. www.ace-cae.eu/fileadmin/New_Upload/7._Publications/Sector_Study/2014/EN/2014_EN_FULL.pdf. Accessed May 21, 2018.

Renner, Michael. 2013. "Global Wage Gap Continues to Widen," *Worldwatch Institute*. January 13. www.worldwatch.org/global-wage-gap-continues-widen-0. Accessed May 21, 2018.

Chapter 37

Property

Architecture would not exist without property. Buildings are the property of an owner, as is the land they occupy and the furniture and equipment they enclose. There exists a long debate over whether property, per se, is natural, something inherent in the way in which we humans occupy this planet, or artificial, something that the state grants us and can take back if it so chooses. As with so many such polarized arguments, the question of whether property is natural or artificial has only one answer: both. Ever since humanity began to occupy permanent settlements and no doubt before then, when we hunted and gathered for our food, people have marked off some part of the landscape as theirs to use and to defend from others, and as such, it seems natural that we humans see the world around us as our property. At the same time, property requires a government of some sort to recognize our ownership of it and to protect it from the theft or vandalism of others, showing how much our property remains an artifice and highly contingent upon an authority able to regulate and police it.

In ethics, this debate lies at the heart of social contract ethics, which considers the duties we have to others in society and what obligations society has to us. Thomas Hobbes argued in the sixteenth century that humans, left to our own devices, will have continual conflicts over property, requiring a strong central authority to keep the peace and adjudicate such matters. For him, the urge to own property may be natural, but its recognition and allocation remained contingent upon the state to decide who owns what and who owes what to whom (Hobbes, 1910). In contrast, the seventeenth-century writer Jean-Jacques Rousseau saw property as artificial and also a terrible thing. The desire for individual ownership lured us away from the common ownership that he thought characterized the state of nature (Rousseau, 1910). But unlike Hobbes, Rousseau would have us return to that state of nature and walk away from the conflicts that private property creates.

The divide over the naturalness or the artificiality of property may seem abstract, but it has real bearing on how architects might think about and act on property. Take, for instance, the dispute between Dallas's Nasher

Sculpture Center and the adjacent Museum Tower (Granberry, 2016). Renzo Piano Workshop designed the glass-roofed sculpture center to have rooftop screens that blocked all direct sunlight, protecting the art within and creating an even interior daylight. But the architects Johnson Fain then designed the 42-story Museum Tower to the north, whose curved glass exterior reflected southern light directly into the museum, countering the goal of the museum's original design and damaging both the art within the center and burning the landscape in the sculpture garden that the tower overlooked. The museum had wanted the architects and developer of the tower to alter its exterior enough to prevent the direct reflections, while the developer and architects of the tower claimed that city approved the design and that it met all code requirements.

Here, the property rights of one owner negatively affected the property of another. While the law acknowledges that one owner does not have the right to damage the property of another, what constitutes damage and where responsibilities lie when a property meets the letter – if not the spirit – of

Figure 37.1 The Museum Tower in Dallas seems innocuous enough until we look at the negative effect it has had on the sculpture center next door, whose interior and exterior spaces have been suffered from the tower's reflections.

the law remains open to question. Municipalities typically deal with such conflicts through zoning regulations and approval processes that, at least in theory, prevent the possibility of one property owner's paradise becoming a neighbor's problem. No law or regulation, however, can anticipate every possible conflict. In this case, the museum tower did not have to change its exterior curtainwall and so the sculpture center made adjustments to mitigate the damage that the tower's reflections caused.

This hardly seems fair: the victim here has to pay for the damages caused by a neighbor. And yet, the tower's architects and developer did not act maliciously since, as the building's name suggests, the museum's proximity served as a major selling point to the people buying condominiums in the high rise. As sometimes happens, though, our desire for proximity to what we most value can end up damaging it in the process. We have seen this with suburbia, in which people's wanting to live close to nature has largely destroyed the natural environment that drew them to the suburbs in the first place. This tower seems like a high-end version of the same paradox. The very act of wanting to overlook the museum and its adjacent sculpture garden brings with it the reflections that threaten to burn the garden's plants and fade the museum's art. Yes, we can have, as William Shakespeare said, "too much of a good thing" (Shakespeare, 1952. p. 618).

The law did not require the tower to alter its design or materials, but social contract ethics would. The museum preceded the tower and so the onus remains with the architect and developer of the tower to fix the reflectance problem they caused. The latter's claim that city approvals give them the right to build the tower as designed remains, if not dishonest, at least disingenuous. The government's approval to carry a fire arm does not give us the right to shoot an innocent bystander, any more than the government's approval of a building gives its developer the right to damage a neighbor's property.

This hiding behind the government's approval of the tower comes at a time when it seems popular to blame the government for almost everything and, at the same time, to starve the government of the funds it needs to do its job, thus giving more cause for blame. No doubt at least some of the wealthy individuals involved in the construction and purchase of the expensive condominiums overlooking the museum would support this anti-government rhetoric as it has become especially popular among those who need the government the least. And yet when wealthy donors to the museum blame the government for not doing more to prevent the reflectance problem, it seems like the height of hypocrisy. People seem to be against the state until they want it to do something that would benefit them.

That also seems self-defeating, as Hobbes and Rousseau recognized with property more generally. The Museum Tower, however efficient its design, lacks utility, in the sense that the consequence of its damage to the

Figure 37.2 The Nasher Sculpture Center is a private institution open to the public, even though the public sector did not protect this institution when negatively affected by an adjacent private property.

adjacent property also conceivably reduces the value of the condominiums it contains. It also lacks virtue, in the sense that it seems unjust that a relatively few wealthy people in the tower get to damage a museum that far more people use, and imprudent, saving money by not fixing the window problem, while paying dearly for the hit to the tower's reputation and that of its developer and architects as a result. The tower might have met the letter of the zoning code, but it violates the social contract that zoning represents. And whatever one might think of its aesthetics, the tower's ethics are ugly indeed.

References

Granberry, Michael. 2016. "Fights, Fantasy Fixes and the FBI: Museum Tower and Nasher still at Odds over Glare after Five Years." *Dallas News*. September 25. www.dallasnews.com/arts/museums/2016/09/25/fights-fantasy-fixes-fbi-museum-tower-nasher-still-odds-glare-five-years. Accessed May 21, 2018

Hobbes, Thomas. 1910. *Of Man, Being the First Part of Leviathan.* The Harvard Classics, Vol. 34. Cambridge: Harvard University Press. 317–434.

Rousseau, Jean-Jacques. 1910. *A Discourse upon the Origin and the Foundation of the Inequality Among Mankind.* The Harvard Classics, Vol. 34. Cambridge: Harvard University Press. 163–234.

Shakespeare, William. 1952. *As You Like It. The Plays and Sonnets of William Shakespeare, Volume One.* Chicago: Encyclopedia Britannica.

Chapter 38

Psychology

As the son of a psychologist, I have found myself, on occasion, having to defend the discipline of psychology among architectural colleagues who see our field as a branch of the arts and humanities and as somehow antithetical to the sciences and social sciences. Although typically thought of as a humanity, ethics has also had to overcome what C.P. Snow called the "two cultures" of the humanities and the sciences, and has begun to embrace the behavioral sciences (Snow, 1998). Architecture needs to do the same. Centrally involved in constructing environments for people, the architectural community still largely ignores environmental psychology, a field that analyzes, among other things, how well the design professions do in meeting people's needs.

Some of this divide has to do with how architects and environmental psychologists communicate. The ways in which the results of psychological research often get conveyed – in dry prose, data tables and descriptive statistics – can turn-off architects accustomed to the visual representation of ideas and information. Likewise, the methodical way in which the behavioral sciences proceed can frustrate architects who have to make many decisions, very rapidly, in the course of doing work. As a result, you hear some architects complain that environmental psychology sometimes seems to discovery the obvious, as some recent research exemplifies: poor children benefit from green space, windows in the workplace improve job satisfaction, aesthetically pleasing stairwells increase their use, and ventilation affects worker performance.

I wonder how much that complaint about environmental psychology serves as a cover for what the design and planning professions have perpetrated on people over the last half century or so, creating cities without enough green space, workplaces without enough windows, offices without adequate ventilation, and stairwells without any appeal. What environmental psychology implicitly reveals is an architectural profession that has been too compliant in accommodating the private sector's rush to maximize profits and the public sector's desire to minimize spending. At the same time, environment-behavior research also seems to show an architectural

Figure 38.1 Offices that have ample daylight, that accommodate physical movement, that encourage interaction, and that accept a diversity of activities, like this co-working space, are often healthier places to work.

discipline that has been overeager to impose its aesthetic ideologies and utopian visions on others, particularly the most vulnerable among us. No wonder many architects do not want to read this literature.

In architecture schools, the argument against environmental psychology among some faculty members has a more philosophical bent. For them, behavior research can seem too deterministic or too simplistic when researchers use the results of their work to drive form-making too directly, without taking into account all of the other factors affecting design. While studio faculty may not hesitate giving students all kinds of other determinants of form, from the building's program to the site's constraints, I think the neglect of social-science research in architecture studios stems from a deeper issue: a suspicion among some academics of a critical-theory persuasion of the empirical, functional, and instrumental orientation of environmental psychology.

This has led to a studio culture in many architecture schools that focuses on propositions more than measurements, aesthetics more than human activity, and speculation more than demonstration. Yet even studio culture has not escaped the attention of environmental psychologists, who have examined studio culture itself and critiqued the lack of diversity there, despite all of the lip service paid to difference in such settings. At the same time, environmental psychologists have analyzed the different world views dividing design and social science. As Irwin Altman and Barbara Rogoff suggest, environmental psychologists lean toward what they call "transactional" worldviews, focusing on the interactions or contexts of people and environments, while designers tend to have "trait" or "organismic" world-views, focusing on the essences or complex wholes of people and places (Altman & Rogoff, 1987).

Despite these different worldviews, research cannot determine what architects do, but it can give practitioners – and clients – reason to do the right things. If anything threatens architects' creativity, it is not environmental psychology, but the relentless cost cutting that characterizes public- as well as private-sector projects. Architects tend to argue against such shortsightedness with generalizations about the effect it will have on people's wellbeing or on the quality of life or the durability of buildings. Environmental behavior research offers another, more powerful argument against clients' cost cutting: it often has negative impacts on human health and productivity, which translate directly into financial losses, which most clients care about a great deal.

Some environmental psychologists have begun to emphasize the natural-environment aspects of the field. These "ecological" psychologists have revealed the sometimes superficial or ineffective ways in which architects have addressed environmental problems, tacking on sustainability as if just one more feature of a building. At the same time, this research suggests that we must see human behavior in its largest possible context – the natural as well as the built environment – if we are to understand not only how

Figure 38.2 Human and environmental health have always been intertwined and the best architecture – like this compact, daylit, naturally cooled, solar powered house – show that a green building is also good to inhabit.

we behave, but the effects that our behavior has on others, humans and nonhumans alike. Environmental psychologists have also focused on social justice issues, which get equally short shrift from many architects.

By looking at the difference that culture, race, gender, and poverty make in the built environment, this research also provides data to back up the critique of power that underlies so much contemporary architectural theory. Indeed, the degree to which psychologists and theorists address many of the same issues, albeit in different ways, makes one wonder if the widespread neglect of environment-behavior research in architectural theory is, itself, a form of power politics, a type of turf protection that some theorists seem to see everywhere else but among themselves.

Not everyone can know everything, and the enormity of the environmental psychology literature can be a deterrent to architects' command of it. Still, that is no excuse for the neglect of this research by too many architects over the last several decades. If nothing else, environmental behavior studies can help us see how much the architecture culture is, itself, an environment in which we behave in often unexamined ways, based on unspoken assumptions, and resulting in unanticipated consequences. Were architects to become more self-conscious and self-critical of our own professional and disciplinary culture, and from the perspective of ethics, more empathetic in our understanding of environmental psychology, we would discover that the latter has much to offer, not least of which is a better understanding of ourselves.

References

Altman, Irwin & Rogoff, Barbara. 1987. "World Views in Psychology: Trait, Interactional, organismic, and transactional perspectives," in D. Stokols & I. Altman (eds.), *Handbook of Environmental Psychology*. New York: Wiley. 7–40.

Snow, C.P. 1998. *The Two Cultures*. Cambridge: Cambridge University Press.

Chapter 39

Public-interest design

After years of serving meals at homeless shelters in my city, I have wondered why the people who would benefit the most from design services have so little access to them. Other professions have figured this out. Medicine gave rise to public health, which attends to the health needs of the entire human population, and law gave rise to legal aid, which addresses the right of all people to seek justice. The design professions, likewise, need to see our responsibility extending beyond the needs of the tiny fraction of clients who have the means to pay our fees, to address the products, services, and shelter needs of people. That stems from the ethical idea that professions, in exchange for the monopoly in the marketplace that licensure allows, have a duty to serve the broadest number of people possible, whether or not they can pay for such services.

This stems from a very practical idea as well. The design professions, especially, continue to overlook an enormous amount of potential work in providing design services for the billions of people on the planet who need what architects and designers can provide. As more and more designers keep competing for an ever-shrinking pool of traditional clients, the time has come for design professionals to rethink our reason for being. Do we really want to continue to be servants of the superrich, or does our responsibility – and our overlooked opportunities for new types of services – also lie with the health, safety, and welfare of all?

This design-for-all philosophy will demand new business models and new forms of architectural education, and possibly even a new profession. The design professions have traditionally followed a medical model of practice, in which the designer addresses a client's particular needs just as a physician does a patient's, supported by an educational system that focuses on creating custom solutions to problems. That model has served the needs of the planet's wealthiest population very well, but it largely leaves out everyone else.

In response to the health needs of underserved populations, the medical profession helped give birth in the mid-nineteenth century to a new profession – public health – to deal with illness and disease within entire populations.

Figure 39.1 The Rocinha favela in Rio de Janeiro shows the contrast between the high-rise towers that architects typically design and the informal settlements whose residents need architectural services as much or more.

Design played a part in the birth of that field, when Frederick Law Olmsted, one of first landscape architects in North America, served as executive secretary of the US Sanitary Commission, which developed recommendations for Union Army camps during America's Civil War. Since then, design and public health have largely gone their separate ways, but that may be changing as the interests of the two fields have once again begun to intersect.

The realignment stems, in part, from some of the major health threats we now face, including chronic diseases, such as obesity and diabetes, that can arise from sedentary lifestyles, and possible pandemic viruses, such as SARS and avian flu, that can come from overcrowded and unsanitary conditions. Designers have played a part in the creation of those conditions: We have contributed directly to the physical inactivity of people in many developed countries through the design of communities that are overly-dependent on cars as a means of transportation, and we have contributed indirectly to the pestilent slums in which much of the world's population now lives by failing to bring our skills to a vast, underserved sector of human society.

To address such issues, we need new business models, different from those of current design practice and more like that of public health. Clients could consist of government groups such as the US Agency for International

Development, intergovernmental organizations such as the World Bank, or private groups such as the Bill & Melinda Gates Foundation. Those organizations already spend billions of dollars annually to improve housing and sanitation in poor countries, so there is no lack of support for the work that needs doing. A public-interest design practice could also tap into a much wider range of colleagues – from public health and technology professionals to cultural consultants – than architects now do. And architects could establish non-profit practices in order to partner with universities and to participate in the research funding available to higher education.

While public-interest designers might still largely provide solutions to the problems of particular places, the scope of the work might involve an entire slum or region of a country, addressing basic needs of shelter, sanitation, clean water, and energy production. Much of the work, though, would probably entail the development of prototypes that could be produced at very low cost in local communities and be carried out by unskilled laborers in myriad cultures and climates. That development, testing, delivery, and continuing evaluation of easily replicable solutions would likely constitute a major portion of the work of public-interest design, which, in turn, would require an education that draws from a wider range of disciplines – anthropology, cultural geography, economics, industrial engineering, public policy – than most design programs now do.

The nature of practice and the scope of education in public-interest design raises the question of whether it could coexist with the existing design fields or if it would constitute a new profession, related to, but distinct from, other forms of design. In one sense, public-interest design encompasses other design fields, such as graphic design, product design, architecture, landscape architecture, and planning, so some knowledge of all of them seems vital. But the focus of design education on the creation of high-cost, resource-intensive solutions to meet the needs of the world's wealthiest, seems largely irrelevant to this new field. Public health separated itself from medicine for similar reasons, and the same may eventually happen with public-interest design and the traditional design fields.

Public-interest design highlights another unmet need for architectural services. Communities and organizations face all sorts of design problems that do not directly involve a building, product, or space: challenges that require paradigm-shifting ways of thinking and working perfectly suited to the problem-solving skills of architects. Services and systems that perform well often just need the tweaking of various management techniques to make them more efficient or effective, but when services and systems become dysfunctional, unaffordable, or unsustainable – which accounts for a growing number conceived in earlier eras under different assumptions – design provides a path toward complete reinvention and real innovation.

This, in turn, could help the architectural profession redefine itself and become more relevant. Just as the legal profession went through a transition

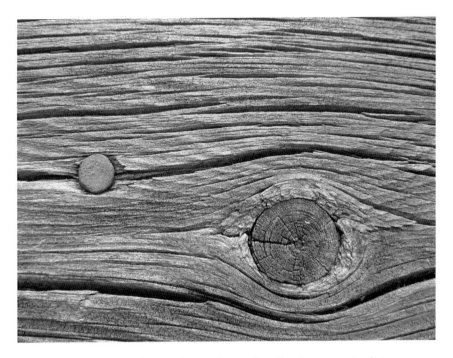

Figure 39.2 Designers work via analogy and metaphor, like the connection between wood knots and the solar system in this photo. Design envisions the future by re-imagining, through analogy, the past and present.

from trial law as the dominant form of legal practice to its being one of many applications of legal thinking, so too might the architectural profession recognize that buildings will become just one of many services practitioners have to offer and that the application of design methods to the vast array of non-building-related problems constitutes one of the greatest unmet needs, and perhaps the greatest growth in demand. Architects essentially help people envision what doesn't yet exist, with the skills required to implement that vision and bring it to fruition. Nowhere in that definition does it require that a building be involved in, or be the answer to, a problem.

Perhaps like law schools, which typically focus on skill development for the first half and the diverse application of those skills in the second half of a student's legal training, architectural schools might do the same: giving students the design thinking and working methods that remain at the core of what an architect does, and then letting students apply those skills differently, in preparation for specialized career paths, from the design of custom buildings for fee-paying clients to mass-customized prototypes for large populations, to system-design services for communities and organizations.

Some might see that as a dilution of the field, but I see it as just the opposite, expanding the field to where the most urgent work needs to be done. And given the millions of people around the world living in unsafe or insecure settings, there is more than enough important work to be done; we have only to figure out how to prepare for it, practice it, and make a profession of it. The design process lets us envision futures that do not yet exist, and so the creation of a new version of ourselves, a field that does not yet exist, should be within our ability to do. We should seize the opportunity before us, go where we are most needed, and do what we do best.

Chapter 40

Quid pro quos

The ethics of a quid pro quo – this for that – depends upon the intention behind the exchange. Barter economies rely upon quid pro quos, in which two sides of a trade determine the equivalency of various goods or services and agree to their exchange, enhancing the ability of people to meet their needs and to engage in beneficial social interactions. Bribery represents a less salubrious example. When a lobbyist donates to a political campaign or does a favor for an elected official with the expectation of an advantageous policy decision in return, the quid pro quo involves corruption and illegal, or at least unethical, practices. While duty ethics would have us focus on the intention behind an exchange, consequentialist ethics would want us to attend to the effects of it: Was it fair and proportional, or did it seek an unfair advantage or disproportionate influence?

The difficulty of answering such a question shows why quid pro quos present some of the most difficult ethical challenges, and ones that professionals and practitioners encounter all the time. Let me give an architectural example. A university ranks design and construction firms pursuing projects at the institution not only according to their skill and experience, but also according to how much money they had contributed in support of students, either through scholarships or internships. Some in the construction industry might look at this as part of the cost of doing business, but others – especially some architects – have refused to work for the institution because they see this practice as both corrupt and corrupting. While explicit bribery has become illegal, at least in more developed parts of the world, quid pro quos have not, since they rarely involve the direct exchange of money and instead revolve around influencing those in power, something very hard to police.

The quid pro quo of this university favoring donors for commissions has an understandable motive. Rising tuition numbers and declining public support for higher education have led many colleges and universities to search for other forms of revenue in order to balance their books, and donations from alumni and supporters of an institution have become one of the most important sources of additional income. Making such donations one

Figure 40.1 Many private institutions favor wealthy alumni and, although not the university in question, Kenyon College has a number of buildings, such as its Science Quad, designed by its wealthy alumnus, architect Graham Gund.

of the criteria for getting work at the university might even appear to have a Robin-Hood-like character, taking from the rich to give to the poor.

But however understandable the motive, the quid pro quo here involves not an equal exchange between peers, but instead an unequal one among parties in which one has most of the power – the university granting the commissions – and others, relatively little of it. This quid pro quo also exacerbates inequities within the construction industry, where large-scale contractors or developers may have more fungible assets to give to the university than design professionals, whose assets lie more in their expertise and experience than in having a lot of cash on hand. One architectural firm I know felt torn by the situation. Should they acquiesce to the university's quid pro quo, as many of contractors had done, or challenge it as both unfair and self-defeating, since the university will not get the best work from its consultants – or even the best consultants – if donations to the institution were a primary criterion for designer selection. And should they protest the university's policy if it might sound as if they did not care about helping students or making higher education more affordable, or should they simply refuse to participate in a practice they opposed?

This raises the age-old ethical question of whether or not the ends, however good, justify the means, however bad. Philanthropy, of course, always involves a degree of pressure applied by those seeking a gift from those who have the capacity to give. That pressure, though, almost always takes the form of playing upon a donor's allegiance to the institution, eagerness to help others, or desire to be recognized or remembered in some permanent way, and such giving remains a voluntary act, which is key. Making the receipt of a commission contingent upon a gift kills the love – the "philo" in philanthropy – and it doesn't say much for its humanity – the "anthropy" – either.

Situations like this, though, highlight the limits of modern ethics. A utilitarian might argue that ranking firms based on the amount of scholarship money they give disadvantages a few – the owners of a firm – in order to benefit many – the generations of students who will receive the scholarship. If some arm-twisting is needed to get firms to give to important institutions that maybe they should have given to anyway, what difference does it make in the utilitarian's calculus of what constitutes the greatest good?

At the same time, a Kantian might argue that the good intention of the institution to help students in need makes this policy acceptable, however objectionable the means of doing so (Kant, 2016). If doing the right thing is what defines the good, and the university is doing so on behalf of students who need the financial support of people who have the means, then the consequences – from a Kantian perspective – do not matter. And if, as Kant would say, we treat everything as if it were to become universal, then making donations a part of how universities award commissions would become something firms would simply figure into their fees, and probably recoup on the back end if they get the job after all.

But good ends or good intentions do not justify any means. Social contract ethics helps us see that extortion must remain outside the bounds of what we consider ethical, lest we create a condition in which bribery and extortion became an expected aspect of trade, a practice that we see happening in some corrupt countries and that has the paradoxical effect of impoverishing everyone as the few in power enrich themselves in the process. A society in which no good deed happens voluntarily means that only bad ones will.

Likewise, virtue ethics enables us to spot the moral flaw in this university's policy. It is neither fair nor just to those competing for work, since it favors the rich over the poor, regardless of talent or ability, something that some institutions practice when giving preference to the children of alumni or donors. Nor is it a prudent policy, since it creates ill will that

Figure 40.2 The Nazis epitomized the evil of quid pro quos, in which an architect like Albert Speer sought favor with those in power. His bombastic buildings, like this Zeppelin grandstand, show the results of such corruption.

costs the institution far more in terms of a ruined reputation than any amount of money it might attract. In any society, when philanthropy becomes misanthropy, all is lost.

Reference

Kant, Immanuel. 2016. *The Collected Works of Immanuel Kant*. London: Delphi Classics.

Chapter 41

Resource use

I have long wondered why architects, economists, and ecologists do not interact more often, since the three fields share an origin in the idea of home. For architects that seems obvious, since a sizable number of design professionals design houses, but the idea of home remains just as relevant to economists and ecologists, who have the Greek word for home – "eco" – in their discipline's name. If architects attend to the homes in which we live, ecologists and economists study and manage the resources of our global home: the earth.

These three fields might benefit from more interaction simply because we all need to do a better job connecting what we do in our personal homes and our planetary one. Any one house, however wasteful or excessive it might be in its use of energy or other resources, may not have much of an impact on the planet, but the cumulative effect of a rapidly growing human population, with millions of people in need of a home, has had an effect on both the global climate as well as the supply of finite resources such as oil and natural gas. We cannot manage our planetary home without a better sense of how our actual homes affect it, and what paradoxes arise as a result.

One such paradox has to do with the fact that, despite all of the good work that has happened to ensure that buildings use less energy, humanity as a whole has been consuming energy at an ever-greater rate. The more efficient we become, the more profligate as well. The British economist William Stanley Jevons saw this happening in the mid-nineteenth century, when he showed that with the greater efficiency in the use of coal came an increase in the rate at which people used coal. This became known as Jevons paradox: that efficiency increases rather than decreases resource use (Polimeni et al, 2008).

Jevons did not just observe this paradox; he also explained why it happens. Greater efficiency in the use of a resource can reduce its price, which prompts more consumption, and it can also increase economic growth, which also fuels greater use as more people can afford to do so. Jevons argued that because of this paradox, we cannot rely on improvements in efficiency alone to reduce consumption of a finite resource. Other factors

Figure 41.1 This still image from the film CCS: a 2 degree solution by Carbon Visuals helps us see the amount of coal humans consumed every day in 2013 – 21.6 million metric tons per day – even as energy efficiency had improved (World Business Council for Sustainable Development, 2015).

need to be put into play to counter the tendency to overuse lower-priced products, which in the case of fossil fuels, includes environmental as well as ethical considerations.

Architects confront Jevons' paradox constantly. Energy-efficient buildings, while reducing fossil fuel consumption in the structure itself, have done little to curb the on-going increase in consumption globally. The same happens with a finite resource such as space – as houses have gotten more efficient in their use of space, the average amount of space in a home in many countries has increased – and like water: as buildings have become more water resourceful, water use globally continues to rise. This does not mean that architects should no longer care about the efficient use of resources; instead, it means that architects – like economists and ecologists – need other ways to curb growing demand.

Some economists might argue that financial mechanisms, such as taxes, quotas, or user fees, will take care of this, just as some ecologists urge the development of public policies that regulate or outright prohibit the wasteful use of finite resources. But such strategies have proven to be hard to sell politically, striking some as "social engineering" and others as tampering with the marketplace, even though, at least in capitalist countries, we seem driven to increase consumption of resources until they become scarce enough that their price rises to a point of maximum returns. We exhaust the very things we most want, as Jevons paradox shows.

Ethics, though, offers another less technical or political way of countering this paradox. One of the primary divisions between ancient and modern ethics has to do with being versus doing. The ancients focused on what it meant to be a good person or on the nature of a good society, while we moderns have tended to dwell, instead, on what it means to do the right thing, regardless of or because of its consequences. Jevons paradox focuses on our "doing," on saving and consuming resources, and has nothing to say about "being" – being a person who doesn't want or need to consume more, for example, regardless of the price or availability of a resource.

The ancient Stoic philosophers argued that our freedom and happiness come not from how much we have, but rather from how much we can do without (Pigliucci, 2017). Consuming more of a finite resource not only potentially harms the planet; according to the Stoics, it also shows how far we have strayed from living according to nature and how far we remain from achieving happiness. Viewed from a modern ecological perspective, humanity's tendency to over-consume resources to the point of their exhaustion

Figure 41.2 This replica of Henry David Thoreau's cabin reflects his Stoic advice that we should measure our wealth according to how much we can do without and that we should live in accord with nature as much as possible.

also demonstrates how much our species – a relatively young and immature species – has yet to learn from others more mature than us in terms of stewarding the resources upon which we depend.

Human beings once did this well, prior to the industrial revolutions. Our hunter-gatherer ancestors knew how to live with little impact on the land and to nurse the resources upon which they depended, leaving little or no trace of their occupation behind. But over the last few centuries, especially, we seem to have forgotten how to do this, another paradox given the amount of information available to us in the digital age. We seem driven to get as much as we can for as little as possible, regardless of the long-term consequences, as Jevons paradox shows.

Were we to attend not to our needs, but that of our home – our personal or planetary one – we would make very different decisions, ensuring that we protect the resources we depend on rather than exhaust them. And were we to understand more deeply what brings us the greatest happiness and freedom, we would seek to live with less and to cultivate our relationships and our own knowledge and virtue instead. Maybe the real paradox in Jevons observation has to do with this modern disconnect between what we think we want, which seems endless, and what we truly need, which requires very few resources. For architecture, economics, and ecology, that means rethinking what we mean by home, and how little it takes to sustain a home.

References

Pigliucci, Massimo. 2017. *How to Be a Stoic: Using Ancient Philosophy to Live a Modern Life*. New York: Basic Books.

Polimeni, John, Mayumi, Kozo Giampietro, Mario & Alcott, Blake. 2008. *The Jevons Paradox and the Myth of Resource Efficiency Improvements*. New York: Routledge.

World Business Council for Sustainable Development. 2015. www.carbonvisuals. com/projects/wbcsd. Accessed July 31, 2018.

Chapter 42

Sexism

We had eight women among the 80 students in my first year in architecture school and I watched as some of those women had to put up with the sexism of one faculty member, who was convinced that they did not belong in what was still a male-dominated profession, and the predatory peccadillos of another, who deluded himself into thinking that the women in my class found him the least bit attractive. I look back on those years, astonished at what men in power got away with. While I would not wish such sexism and sexual harassment on anyone, I do wonder what might change if every man experienced what women do all the time and knew what it felt like to be the focus of unwanted attention. I suspect this would result in much less harassment of all sorts.

The situation of women in architecture has only marginally improved since then. While universities have gotten better at policing the sexual harassment of students on the part of faculty, and while women have almost reached parity with men in terms of the numbers of students in architecture programs, architecture itself lags behind other fields in becoming a more female-friendly profession. In the US, for example, the proportion of women architecture students has hit 43%, a far cry from the 10% in my class. But the number of women who work in the field remains much lower, 24%, and the number of licensed women architects even lower, 14% (ACSA, 2014).

Something happens after women graduate from school, when those who have excelled in school for various reasons do not make it through the internship process or decide not to get licensed. This doesn't reflect a lack of opportunity for women. Many public-sector and even a number of private-sector clients give preference to hiring women-owned, as well as minority-owned businesses as part of their design teams, in an effort to encourage such under-represented groups. Many architecture and design firms also actively seek a diverse work force and make concerted efforts to recruit women to their offices. At the same time, women continue to make major contributions to the design world, producing much of the very best work.

The problem lies elsewhere: in a profession that is perennially underpaid and overworked in relation to the value it creates and the liability it assumes.

Figure 42.1 Elizabeth Diller, the first architecture recipient of a MacArthur Foundation "genius" award, straddles the fields of architecture and philosophy, producing thought-provoking architecture that often raises profound philosophical questions.

And therein lies an irony. The very institutions trying to create opportunities for under-represented groups also sometimes create the conditions that lead women and minorities to leave the profession because of the relatively low pay and the long hours required to do the work. In that sense, the lack of women as licensed architects serves as a warning and a symptom of a larger dilemma that many in the field seem unwilling to talk about: the devaluation of the design professions perpetrated by those in power.

Philosophy faces a similar dilemma. A foundational field that in some sense underpins every other, philosophy, too, remains under-valued in the marketplace and mistakenly viewed as impractical as a career. Philosophy majors, for example, have starting salaries comparable to those in many other fields and they have, on average, an increase in their mid-career salary higher than most others (Lam, 2015). At the same time, women remain under-represented in philosophy, with numbers similar to those in architecture: a 2007 study by the philosopher Sally Haslanger revealed that women accounted for only 18.7% of those in tenure-track positions in philosophy departments and only 12.36% of the authors of articles in the top philosophy journals (Haslanger, 2007).

The sexism in both fields may stem, in part, from their common origin in ancient Greece, where sexist attitudes against women took root among its major thinkers, all male, as the philosopher Vigdis Songe-Møller has shown (Songe-Møller, 2002). And the male dominance in both architecture and philosophy continued with the central role they played in constructing, physically and intellectually, the structures of the medieval period and the subsequent era of aristocratic rule, when misogyny reigned.

That history in no way excuses the sexism in both fields, but it does highlight the paradox of its continued prevalence. The design of a building and the conception of an ethical argument begins with an understanding of the needs of others, be it the physical space needs of the occupants or the obligational space needs of people in some sort of relationship with each other. These fields, of course, did not always see this as their starting point. For centuries architects have imposed forms, just as philosophers have imposed systems on people in a more or less procrustean manner. But in this post- or post-post-modern period, we no longer accept such impositions, and any field that doesn't begin with an empathetic understanding of the situation of others will not stand.

Which makes the eradication of sexism in architecture and in philosophy so essential. It is not only long overdue, it is also a measure of whether these fields remain viable going forward. People will still need shelter and still engage in thought, so the functions of these fields will endure, but whether they continue in their current form is a question worth considering. In architecture, for example, the emergence of public-interest design points to a very

Figure 42.2 Lookout Studio at the Grand Canyon was designed in the 1920s by architect Mary Colter, one of the many under-appreciated women architects of her day, doing work sensitive to context and cultures.

different form of education and practice, one in which the architect engages people regardless of their ability to pay, in the place in which they live, and uses the materials and means at their disposal in order to help them meet their needs as they define them. The "ethical turn" in many fields, from psychology to anthropology to literary theory, represents a similar movement in ethics (Davis & Womack, 2001). As Kant would say, this trend treats people – men and women – as ends in themselves and not means to our ends as professionals.

The era of the architect as the heroic form-giver and the philosopher as the visionary system-builder has come to an end, whether those who still hold to those outdated notions know it or not. And with it goes the misogyny and inequality that those fields have embraced, consciously or not, since ancient Greece. In their place have begun to emerge new versions of architecture and philosophy based on web-like ways of thinking and working, in which practitioners of these disciplines facilitate connections, enable access, and enhance equity as fundamental to how we act and interact. The demand for gender equity helped open the door to this way of being and it is a threshold that we all need to cross.

References

ACSA (Association of Collegiate Schools of Architecture). 2014. "Where are the Women? Measuring Progress on Gender in Architecture." www.acsa-arch.org/resources/data-resources/women. Accessed May 21, 2108.

Davis, Todd & Womack, Kenneth. 2001. *Mapping the Ethical Turn: A Reader in Ethics, Culture, and Literary Theory*. Charlottesville: University of Virginia Press.

Haslanger, Sally. 2007. "Changing the Ideology and Culture of Philosophy: Not by Reason (Alone)." Department of Linguistics and Philosophy, Massachusetts Institute of Technology. www.mit.edu/~shaslang/papers/HaslangerWomeninPhil07.pdf. Accessed May 21, 2108.

Lam, Bourree. 2015. "The Earning Power of Philosophy Majors," *The Atlantic*. September 3. Washington DC.

Songe-Møller, Vigdis. 2002. *Philosophy without Women: The Birth of Sexism in Western Thought*. New York: Continuum.

Chapter 43

Space

Because ethics so rarely got discussed in architecture school, I decided to study ethics as part of my graduate education and found that a grounding in the built environment helped a great deal in my understanding of moral philosophy. Knowing about architects such as Ludwig Mies van der Rohe and Frank Lloyd Wright helped me comprehend – and critique – Hegel's ideas (Hegel, 2001). Likewise, reading Hegel's critics helped me see the limitations of what Mies and Wright and so many other modern architects proposed: not every thesis and antithesis leads to a new synthesis, as Hegel argued; sometimes one extreme begets its opposite and the two remain in perpetual polarization, as we know from the modernist and classicist camps in architecture today.

What surprised me in my pursuit of ethics was how rarely the ethics literature ever mentioned the built environment. In some cases, ethical philosophy took its name from the places in which it occurred: The Stoics, for example, practiced their inquiries into how to live according to nature in the open walkways or porticos of the ancient world, called Stoa. But much of the ethics of the Greeks and Romans focused on the cultivation of a virtuous character, which made the physical space in which this occurred less important than the intellectual and emotional "space" of a person. Indeed, the Stoics argued, despite the architectural origin of their name, that the material world around us and the physical needs and desires of our bodies have little to do with our happiness, which lies, instead, in the cultivation of our virtue and in our living according to nature.

It wasn't until the rise of social contract ethics in seventeenth-century Europe, with its focuses on the nature of a good society, that the physical, social, and political context of ethics became more prominent. Thomas Hobbes envisioned a social contract in which a strong authority would keep people from engaging in the war of all against all, with an engraving showing this Leviathan leader towering above a city and its surrounding countryside that captures the spatial quality of his ideal commonwealth. In Jean-Jacques Rousseau's social contract, small city states enable democracy to flourish since their leaders remain closer to, and more accountable to, the

Figure 43.1 This image on the title page of Thomas Hobbes's 1651 book, *Leviathan*, shows how he was thinking about ethics and the social contract in terms of the landscape and space of the city, laid out before the strong ruler.

general will of the people governed. And fictional works involving the social contract, such as Thomas More's *Utopia*, pay equal attention to the spatial aspects of the ideal community, its layout, organization, and operation. While social contract ethics pays a lot of attention to how people interact with each other in particular places, many of its proponents envisioned relatively small communities, with people physically proximate and culturally unified enough to agree on what constitutes good behavior and the right action in a given situation.

The spatial scale of Western ethics began to grow with the rise of deontology or duty ethics in the work of Immanuel Kant. In his universalizing of right and wrong in his categorical imperatives, he made the argument that ethics applies to all people regardless of social position. Treating others as ends and not means to our ends applied, he believed, to every human being and, to some extent, he was right. Except for the rare masochist, we all want to be respected and valued and not treated as someone else's pawn or plaything, but as architects learned in the twentieth century, universalizing a set of ideas can have the opposite effect on people whose values may differ in emphasis or in substance. The International Style, for instance, with its belief that the same glass-and-steel building could be built anywhere and for almost any purpose, echoed the spatial universalism of Kant's ethics, but had the effect of denying the differences of place, culture, and climate and of treating people, not as ends in themselves, but as means to end of architectural ideology. Scale matters in ethics as it does in architecture, and the scale of Kant's ethics and of the International Style's aspirations showed how a good idea, taken too far and applied too broadly, can become a bad one (Kant, 1952).

If the universalizing of ethics got it in trouble, so did its quantification. Jeremy Bentham's utilitarianism sought to calculate the good according to the number who benefited from it, as if the good were some sort of popularity contest or political campaign, up for a vote (Bentham, 1988). Alexis de Tocqueville highlighted one of the shortcomings of that utilitarian calculus in his claim that we have to beware of the tyranny of the majority, a problem particularly relevant to modern democracies, with their winner-takes-all approach to elections (De Tocqueville, 2003). Modern public housing has shown, more recently, another drawback of utilitarian ethics. While such housing may have had good intentions, something that Kant would have appreciated, its effort to produce the greatest number of units for the greatest number of people produced stripped-down buildings and barren landscapes that, in the name of the charity, became poor places in which to live.

Fiascos such as the now-demolished Pruitt-Igoe public housing project in St. Louis demonstrate that we cannot ascertain the greatest good for the greatest number without asking what constitutes the good, who determines it, and who gets counted in that calculation. As I learned, while studying the efforts in Hong Kong of rehousing families living in informal settlements into sterile high-rise apartment buildings, giving people new apartments while breaking up their social bonds and community relationships does them little good and a lot of harm, something that the bureaucrats engaged in this rehousing effort did not want to acknowledge. They acted as if they knew what was good for families and they measured their achievement by how many families they rehoused, without bothering to ask those most affected by their decisions what they wanted.

If many ethical systems either ignore space or overlook scale, ethical behavior remains space and scale dependent. Many unethical actions, for example, arise from an often-misguided sense on the part of individuals that they can get away with something by thinking that they are immune from and insulated from the consequences of that behavior, in part because of physical or spatial isolation. Out of sight, out of mind. Of course, we occupy the same planet and so the idea of spatial insulation from the effects of our decisions and our actions remains an illusion. We remain linked in so

Figure 43.2 The high-density housing of Hong Kong has greatly improved the living conditions of many of its residents, but sometimes at the price of breaking up the spatial connections among people, central to the maintenance of community.

many ways and we fool ourselves when we think we can ultimately escape the consequences of what we do, however much that might appear to be the case in the short term.

Take global poverty, a topic that people in the developed world may find far removed from their concerns. As we have seen with viruses such as Ebola and Zika, slum conditions may give rise to these pathogens, but global airline travel – often by the richest people on the planet – has enabled the sickness and death that can come from exposure to these germs to spread around the world to the wealthiest parts as well as the poorest. The sense of security that comes with spatial separation becomes quickly undermined by technologies such as airplanes that connect us across vast distances.

Much unethical behavior also arises from looking at the world from our own point of view or in terms of what might benefit us. Ethics, in contrast, helps us see things from others' perspective, which is itself a spatial term. What does the world look like, for example, from the position of a young person or an old one, of a government official or a private individual, and of an owner or renter? Such projective understanding also allows us to do thought experiments, imagining perspectives completely different from our own: what, for example, does the world look like from the point of view of an animal or an ancestor or our progeny? These questions do not lend themselves to precise answers, but they do open up new ways of seeing and acting upon the spaces and times in which we live.

The relative perspectives from which ethics helps us view a situation has led some to argue that ethics remains a matter of opinion rather than something we can assess and agree upon – or at least agree to disagree about. But here, spatial ethics might help us see that claim from, yet again, another perspective. The design process, while involving a fair amount of intuitive responses to a site or situation, does represent a collaborative coming to agreement over what should be done, and in that sense, it represents not a personally subjective position, but rather a collectively interactive one, in which a group of people in a particular place and time decide what makes the most sense within the given constraints. That may change with different people, at a different time, or in a different place, making architecture and ethics less a matter of personal opinion than of spatial opportunities.

References

Bentham, Jeremy. 1988. *The Principles of Morals and Legislation*. New York: Prometheus Books.
De Tocqueville, Alexis. 2000. *Democracy in America*. London: Penguin Books.
Hegel, Georg Wilhelm Friedrich. 2001. *The Philosophy of History*. Kitchener, Ontario: Batoche Books.
Kant, Immanuel. 1952. *The Critique of Practical Reason*. Chicago: Encyclopedia Britannica. Vol 42.

Chapter 44

Student work

Ethics often defines the border between the empathetic understanding of others and their exploitative undermining of them, especially in situations where power differences exist, like those between faculty and students in universities. I know an architect who, when she became the new director of an architecture program, discovered that some faculty members had used their own residences as the sites for students' design/build studios. The director said that this practice had to stop because it constituted a conflict of interest, with faculty members using student labor to increase the value of their property, although the professors involved claimed that the use of their own homes enabled their students to make mistakes and to take risks that they could not otherwise do. They saw it as a learning experience, not as exploitation.

That difference of opinion raised a central issue in ethics: what constitutes the proper – and improper – use of human labor? Adam Smith saw the division of labor as a way of increasing people's productivity and with it, their wealth; through this collective activity, Smith believed, the material conditions of everyone would improve (Smith, 1994). Karl Marx agreed, although he argued that since workers "own" their labor, they should control the process of its deployment and benefit the most from it (Marx, 2009). In Marx's view, a capitalist exploited other people's labor by making them work more than they needed to in order to enrich those who sought to profit by it.

Architecture, of course, has long had a division of labor at its core. Architects design a building, engineers size the structural elements necessary to make it stand and operate, and contractors build from the detailed drawings and specifications. And much of the tension in the construction industry arises from the ethical conflict identified by Smith and Marx. Who should benefit the most from the division of construction-industry labor: the architects and engineers who determine what contractors build without actually doing the construction, or the contractors whose labor is essential to realizing the building? And how does the intellectual labor of design professionals relate to the physical labor of the building trades, a question that has dogged

Figure 44.1 Filippo Brunelleschi straddled the medieval guild system and modern architectural system, designing not just the Florence Cathedral dome, but also the equipment needed to erect it, in a spectacular example of design build.

the construction industry since at least the time of Flippo Brunelleschi who, in the early 1400's broke from the guild system to call himself an architect (Walker, 2002).

A whole system of contracts, codes and regulations arose since then to ensure some degree of fairness in this industry and to prevent the exploitation of people in the process. Contracts ensure that the design team get paid for their work, codes ensure that the safety of people gets protected, and regulations ensure that, at least in public work, trades get paid the prevailing wage. Almost none of these protections exist, however, for the design/build projects students engage in during school. In most cases, students work for credit rather than for pay and create structures as part of a class that rarely gets inspected by code officials. On top of that, the faculty members involved often end up serving in the role of the client, determining the nature and location of the project and deciding upon the grades that individual students will get as a result of their effort.

While design/build studios in school can offer invaluable lessons, such exercises also leave open the possibility of real abuse, as in the case of faculty mentioned above. However much it may give students greater freedom in what they build and more latitude to make mistakes, using student labor to improve professors' own property constitutes the very exploitation that Marx cautioned us about. The faculty members involved not only controlled the application and extent of the students' labor, but also benefited inordinately from the product of that effort.

The professors' protests against the school administrator's admonitions echo those of capitalists in Marx's era. Smart people can always find reasons, whether economic or educational, to justify unethical behavior, something particularly ironic in institutions of higher education when faculty, who often lean to the left politically, end up engaging in activities that characterize the most repressive, right-wing regimes. The new director, here, has no choice but to demand that the faculty members cease and desist, and if they refuse, the director needs to report them, regardless of the personal consequences. Might, in this case, must make things right.

When it comes to students' intellectual labor, however, the ethical issues become less clear. Many schools assert their right to keep samples of student work, necessary as part of the accreditation process, but who retains the rights to that work? Does it become the property of the school or remain that of the student? While architecture has a long and well-established relationship with property, since a building requires that its owner controls the

Figure 44.2 Yale's School of Architecture has long had a first-year design/build studio in which students work, in this case, with Columbus House, a local homeless non-profit, to conceive and construct a house for someone who does not have one.

plot of land on which it stands, the relationship of architecture to intellectual property has less of a history and a much weaker standing.

We can pace out and mark the boundaries of a piece of real estate, but how do we define the boundaries of an idea or a design? We cannot replicate a piece of land; by definition, each parcel of property remains unique and capable of ownership, but given the almost infinite combinations of forms, spaces, materials and products that constitute a building, and the ability to construct replicas of it from the same set of drawings, how much must change in a design before one differs substantially from another?

The home-building industry highlights this problem. That industry depends upon standard home plans, widely available on newsstands and the Internet and available to purchase from the plan providers who hold the intellectual property of their designs. At the same time, home builders constantly modify those plans to fit particular site conditions or home-owners' needs, and at what point does that become a new design, a unique piece of intellectual property capable of replication without having to pay the original plan provider?

This question becomes even more complicated when considering the intellectual property of many students. In a design/build project, for example, when several students work on one structure, it becomes almost impossible to say who among them owns the intellectual property. Which student's ideas define the unique characteristics of the design? And do they know, for certain, that no one else has ever come up with essentially the same design, since architecture – unlike inventions – almost never gets patented? The primary protection of a design comes not from the patent office but from its being a unique response to a particular site and client and so, almost by definition, unrepeatable.

Which applies to students as well as buildings. Rather than see students as cheap labor or free idea generators, universities – and the professions – need to treat students as they would anyone else, as individuals who deserve to be paid and credited for their work and as people who have the right to say no to the exploitation of those in power. Not a "reserve army of labor," to use Marx's term, at the beck and call of professors or practitioners, students are free agents whose skills, talents, and intellectual property are theirs to employ – or not (Marx, 2009, pp. 311–317).

References

Marx, Karl. 2009. *Das Kapital*. Washington DC: Regnery Publishing.
Smith, Adam. 1994. *The Wealth of Nations*. New York: Random House.
Walker, Paul Robert. 2002. *The Feud that Sparked the Renaissance*. New York: HarperCollins.

Chapter 45

Style

Earlier in my career, I lived through the style wars, the battles that modernists, postmodernists, classicists, and deconstructionists waged over the aesthetics of their buildings. Modern architects argued that the modern era had not ended and that we still lived in a time of mass-produced, machine-made products, which defined our buildings as well, while deconstructionists responded that such a master narrative marginalized those who were outliers and obscured the actual contradictions and power relations that exist in the world. Meanwhile, the postmodernists pointed to the historical contradictions of modernism and how it represented just one more style in a long line of architectural expression, and the classicists went even further to say that modernism remained an aberration in an otherwise continuous evolution of classical architecture.

Such style wars have settled down and, as often happens with wars, I look back at them now and wonder why we even bothered to fight them. Given the other social and environmental challenges we face, does it really matter all that much whether or not a building has a pitched roof, a classical column or a modernist one? Have we entered a time when we need "Less Aesthetics, More Ethics", as the Venice Biennale organized by architect Massimiliano Fuksas put it, with less of a focus on appearances and more of a focus on actions that tangibly improve peoples' lives and the health of the planet? (Fuksas, 2000). Such thoughts were on my mind when, on a visit to Cambridge University on business, I saw a poster promoting a conversation about styles in ethics. I had not thought about there being styles of ethics, at least not like the styles of architecture, and I wondered if ethicists had fought over their styles as fiercely as architects? What, I wondered, constituted an ethical style and what, if anything, do ethical styles and architectural styles have to do with each other?

That question led me to look up an essay by the philosopher Bertrand Russell, once a professor at Cambridge University, entitled "Styles in Ethics" (Russell, 2009). At the time, the essay must have roiled some people, since it questioned, among other things, whether there existed any absolutes regarding sexual morality and the institution of marriage. But more to the point,

Russell, a philosopher who admired the precision of science and math, dismissed in his essay ethics itself as unquantifiable and thus "the business of the mystic, the artist and the poet," just a matter of "style" (Russell, 2009, p. 326). To a mathematically inclined mind like Russell's, style might have seemed superficial or subjective. However, as the buildings of Cambridge amply demonstrate, style also tells us a lot about the individuals and communities of people who create something, reflecting their view of the world and their manner of expression.

And in this regard, ethics and architecture seem aligned. The Gothic architecture of Cambridge colleges such as Kings, Queens, Trinity, and Clare struck me as a reflection, in stone, of the medieval emphasis on virtues such as faith, hope, and charity. The statues of notable thinkers or patrons from the past on such buildings and the monstrous gargoyles spouting water during storms bring to mind the ancient and medieval view of ethics as a process of character development and the inculcation of good habits, as well as the reminder of what we can become – monsters – when we neglect such self-improvement. While Russell might point out how much we have superseded Aristotle's view of science, the latter's view of ethics as the cultivation of virtue and moderation of our excesses – including Russell's extreme skepticism – remains as relevant today as the medieval colleges at Cambridge.

Likewise, Cambridge's classical buildings have a very different style as did the ethics of the era in which they were built, rife with political and religious conflicts. In Wren's library at Trinity, with its clever disguise of the

Figure 45.1 Christopher Wren's library at Trinity College shows how form and function had begun to separate in the early modern era, with the exterior and interior floor levels not aligned, for aesthetic and practical reasons.

reading room volume behind a wall of classical columns imposed across the façade, you can see in stone the social-contract ethics of a thinker such as of Thomas Hobbes, who viewed a good society as an orderly one, in which individual differences and conflicts get suffused within a larger whole. And you can see in the symmetrical compositions and balanced proportions of the classical buildings such as James Gibbs' Senate House a visual equivalent of John Locke's social contract in which checks and balances curb the natural tendency of people to seek absolute power or excessive control. The political ethics that have guided so many modern democracies seem to have their equivalent in the architectural aesthetics of those structures.

At the same time, the Cambridge colleges built and added to throughout the late eighteenth and nineteenth centuries seem to echo, stylistically, the ethics of Kant from that same period. Kant's emphasis on our duty to do the right thing, regardless of the possible negative consequences to ourselves, seems evident in the deference that eighteenth-century architects paid to each other's buildings at Cambridge, with new structures continuing the language, materials, and cornice heights of the adjacent ones (Kant, 2016). Kant's focus on good intentions also seems equivalent to the well-intended efforts among the architects of Cambridge to ply their building's walls with quotations that exhort us to pursue our better selves.

The ethical and architectural style tour continues into the twentieth century with buildings such as Giles Gilbert Scott's Cambridge's University Library, which provides access to books on such a vast scale that it seems to embody the utilitarian idea that the quantity of a good thing trumps other qualities. The library's stripped-down Classicism seems to mirror the sentiment of doing so as efficiently as possible, without the weight of tradition getting in its way. And the growing skepticism about ethics, which we heard in Russell's essay, has its architectural equivalent in later twentieth-century Cambridge buildings as well. James Stirling's structure for the history department, for example, looks more like a factory building than one intended for faculty, with steel trusses and glass walls whose technical qualities echo Russell's affinity for science and his dismissal of style as something for poets, not professors.

Stirling's design, of course, has a style, as does everything we create, whether or not we acknowledge it. The question we face in the twenty-first century is whether we can stop arguing over style and get on with the work that ethics and architecture have to do, which is how to construct a better world than the one we have now. At the same time, simply dismissing style as unimportant doesn't seem satisfactory either since, as Cambridge shows, buildings embody the ideas, aspirations, and values of their time as do their architects who, however idiosyncratic or original they may be, still swim in the culture and era in which they work and who cannot help but reflect that in their work.

It matters that a work has a style since, as a work produced in a particular place and time, by and for particular people, it will embody what

Figure 45.2 The industrial character of James Stirling's History Faculty at Cambridge reflects the scientism that had overtaken many disciplines in the twentieth century, including architecture as well as humanities like history.

observers, often years later, see as a characteristic style of an era and the people behind it. That does not occur in any linear way; cultures and communities can cycle back to earlier eras, as we saw Renaissance artists do with the Classical predecessors. And it still happens today as we watch architects such as Robert A.M. Stern create new colleges for Yale University that echo in plan and in image the Gothic-style colleges built at Yale in the 1930s. Utilizing the most advanced digital and pre-fabrication technology, Stern's firm fabricated buildings that would look at home in medieval England, all of which suggests that style may not matter as much as doing something well.

Which also begins to answer the question: How do we know if our work has style? We may admire the style of others and try to emulate or even copy it in our own work, and we may acquire certain ways of doing things that follow the ideas of others, becoming part of a movement or architectural style. But the attribution of style has to come from others, not from ourselves. This can come from contemporary critics who see in the work connections to that of others and who assess the meaning of those connections as part of a larger trend. Or it can come from historians, years from now, who have the perspective to see in the results a tendency or approach that characterizes a person's body of work or an era's identifiable features. So, does your work have style? Yes, but that is not for you to say.

References

Fuksas, Massimiliano. 2000. *Citta: Less Aesthetics, More Ethics*. New York: Rizzoli/ St. Martin's Press.
Kant, Immanuel. 2016. *The Collected Works of Immanuel Kant*. London: Delphi Classics.
Russell, Bertrand. 2009. *Russell: The Basic Writings of Bertrand Russell*. London: Routledge.

Chapter 46

Surveillance

I teach urban design and in virtually every class, my students and I end up talking about the impact of digital technology, asking such questions as: How has our behavior changed as people have eyes glued to their mobile devices as they walk, engaged in digital interactions even as they inhabit a physical space? How has the surveillance of these same spaces become pervasive, creating environments in which our every move gets scrutinized by unseen observers in the name of our safety? And how have these two phenomena – personal devices and pervasive cameras – altered the distinction that used to exist between the public and private, making public space a place of private experience and private conversations an acceptable part of public space?

While the answers to such questions remain unresolved, they raise issues that communities face every day. At my university, for example, the theft of students' electronic devices on and off campus has led the institution to install a sizable number of surveillance cameras on buildings in the area. While some students have welcomed the increased security that this seems to provide, others have argued that the university should, instead, encourage more pedestrian activity, transparent storefronts, and "eyes on the street" to discourage theft and render additional cameras unnecessary.

The ethicist Peter Singer has written insightfully about some of the ethical dilemmas that such situations create (Singer, 2011). In our media-saturated world, where the widespread use of cameras and the apparent urge of people to tell all on their Facebook pages, privacy has almost completely disappeared, he argues. Singer makes his point with an architectural analogy, referring to Jeremy Bentham's Panopticon. Imagined by Bentham as the perfect surveillance device, the Panopticon was a radial building in which one person could stand at the center and observe the activities of everyone at the perimeter.

Singer observes that:

> The modern Panopticon is not a physical building . . . With surveillance technology like closed-circuit television cameras and digital cameras

now linked to the Internet, we have the means to implement Bentham's inspection principle on a much vaster scale. What's more, we have helped construct this new Panopticon, voluntarily giving up troves of personal information. We blog, tweet, and post what we are doing, thinking and feeling.

(Singer, 2001, pp. 32–36)

His argument reminds me of a comment that an audience member made in a computer conference, in which she noted that while we associate our digital devices with personal freedom, few technologies provide a better tool for a dictatorial regime to track and control people than these. We occupy this political Panopticon, whether or not we blog or tweet.

Key to the ethics of this "modern Panopticon" is the question of whether we participate in it voluntarily or not. When we choose to go into public places, we give up a degree of privacy in order to be with or interact with other people, in what the philosopher Hannah Arendt called "the space of appearance," which she recognized as an ephemeral and fragile phenomenon that depends upon our willingness to continue to participate in public

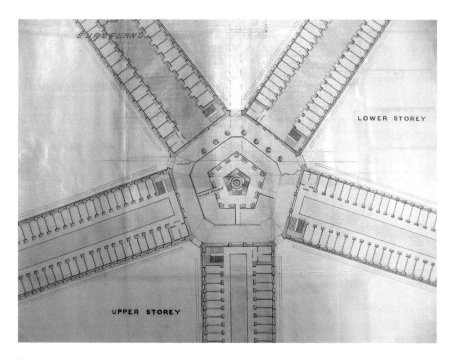

Figure 46.1 Jeremy Bentham's design of a Panopticon represented the architectural equivalent of total surveillance, in which a guard at the center could watch all of the inmates, who couldn't tell if they were being watched or not, and altered their behavior accordingly.

life (Arendt, 1958, p. 199). In our era, that public participation also means our acceptance of being monitored by surveillance cameras. While some on my campus complain that a security camera violates their privacy, their appearance in public means that they have already relinquished a degree of privacy, whether observed by cameras or by other people.

That claim, though, does reflect a widespread misunderstanding of, and indeed an unfortunate decline in, public life and the public realm. Busy streets, full of pedestrians able to watch for possible criminal behavior, can make cameras irrelevant, which is what those who argued for an enlivened campus in lieu of cameras had in mind. Meanwhile the lack of such crowds has not only prompted the electronic surveillance of public spaces, but also perhaps set in motion a downward spiral in which people turn to the digital public space of social media in lieu of a physical interaction with others who may be different from, or disagree with, us.

Social contract theory has some relevance here. Thomas Hobbes argued that we need a strong central authority to keep people from harming each other, as he believed we would do without such restraint. He would likely have supported the use of surveillance cameras on campus for that reason (Hobbes, 1910). Jean-Jacques Rousseau, in contrast, had a suspicion of central authority and believed people to be naturally good apart from the corrupting influence of society, and he would probably have argued the fewer cameras, the better (Rousseau, 1910).

Between those two extreme views stood John Locke, who recognized the value of central authority but argued that its legitimacy rests with the consent of the governed (Locke 1952). Locke might have urged the university to find a balance between deploying cameras where absolutely necessary and doing whatever possible to encourage people to assemble in public. Singer's essay echoes Locke. Singer observes that electronic devices now allow those surveyed to watch their surveyors as well as the other way around. Such two-way surveillance becomes analogous to democracy, in which we, the governed, watch our representatives, protecting not only our security, but also our liberty.

This seems especially relevant to universities. These institutions have a responsibility not only to research and reflect upon the impact of technology, but also to question our assumptions about it, to balance competing interests, and to respect the privacy of individuals, however quaint that may sound to some. Security personnel may not want their cameras visible, so that thieves don't simply move their criminal activity to other, less-surveyed places. But letting students survey the surveyors, making sure that the information gathered does not get misused, becomes a crucial step in any surveillance effort.

At the same time, architects have a responsibility to raise such issues with clients and communities. While some number of security cameras will invariably remain a part of our built environment, design can make a huge difference in how people behave in public. Buildings might combine defensible

Figure 46.2 Pervasive surveillance cameras in the built environment has made public life not just a spatial phenomenon that occurs in physical space, but a temporal one as well, with those actions kept forever on file.

space and protective perimeters that make potential thieves more obvious with an internal openness and transparency that makes a possible theft more apparent. This does not mean constructing a physical version of Singer's new Panopticon. Safety stems not from depending upon paid personnel occupying some central observation post, but instead from accepting our mutual responsibility for our collective security, even if this means looking up on occasion from our mobile devices and caring for each other's wellbeing.

References

Arendt, Hannah. 1958. *The Human Condition*. Chicago: University of Chicago Press.

Hobbes, Thomas. 1910. *Of Man, Being the First Part of Leviathan*. The Harvard Classics, Vol. 34. Cambridge: Harvard University Press, 317–434.

Locke, John. 1952. *Concerning Civil Government*. Chicago: University of Chicago Press, Vol. 35.

Rousseau, Jean-Jacques. 1910. *A Discourse upon the Origin and the Foundation of the Inequality Among Mankind*. The Harvard Classics, Vol. 34. Cambridge: Harvard University Press. 163–234.

Singer, Peter. 2011. "Visible Man: Ethics in a World without Secrets," *Harpers*. August. 32–36.

Chapter 47

Terrorism

Ethical insights often come from the most unethical actions, and that seems to be the case with terrorism. Killing innocent people to make a political or religious statement remains among the most heinous and unethical acts imaginable and yet, we can also learn from terrorists. They continually look for ways to take advantage of vulnerabilities in our systems and so they force us to consider what we have most neglected, be it the protections that

Figure 47.1 The temporary light memorial to the lives lost in the World Trade Center was not only aesthetically powerful, but also ethically compelling in its use of searchlights as a sign of being on high alert against the next attack.

ensure our safety or the unanticipated connections among seemingly unrelated phenomena in our physical world. While we have made skyscrapers and airplanes safe as independent systems, for example, we had not considered what would happen if someone intentionally intersected the two, flying a plane full speed into a tower, as happened on 9/11.

The ethical questions this raises are two-fold. On one hand, terrorism causes us to ask how far we will compromise our freedom in the name of security. Since 9/11, security has tended to win out as people frightened by terrorism have accepted everything from widespread surveillance to political extremism in response to the perceived threat, even though we face a greater likelihood of suffering a lightning strike than a terrorist attack. While individuals have a right to strike that balance in their own lives, the imposition of one person's unfounded fears on others through the people they vote into power and the laws that then get passed represents an abrogation of our collective freedom to decide for ourselves how much security we need. This, of course, is exactly what terrorists want: to inflict dread that exceeds the actual peril and that leads us to oppress ourselves in ways they never could. Terrorism, in other words, shows how one unanticipated unethical act can breed many self-imposed ones.

Another ethical dilemma that terrorism raises has to do with how transparent we are in responding to it. Those who would keep our terrorism response secrete argue, understandably, that we do not want to tip our hand, but terrorists rarely do what has worked in the past and move on to new vulnerabilities, so transparency will not likely increase the threat. If anything, transparent communication can work in our favor by sending messages that can confuse terrorists and reduce the likelihood of their attack, making them unsure of whether or not we have anticipated their actions.

An architect described one example of what this might look like. A client of a high-rise building in a country with hostile neighbors asked this architect's firm to design a disguised anti-missile installation at the top of the tower. While the architect felt obliged to accommodate the client – and the country's – request, it raised questions about whether or not the inhabitants of the building should know about the installation and also about how people would feel working in what would become a possible military target. Safety ranks, along health and welfare, as one of the primary responsibilities of architects, but design professionals often think of safety in terms of ensuring the stability of a structure, the accessibility of fire exits, and the security of every element in a building – not often in terms of protecting a facility from terrorism.

Since 9/11, an air-borne strike at a building has become a definite possibility, particularly if the structure carries symbolic importance to an enemy. As a result, the design of especially high-rise or high-security structures now often includes a simulation of how the building would withstand a direct hit by, say, an airplane fully loaded with fuel. Installing anti-missile devices in a building that doesn't otherwise have a military purpose seems to take this to another level, however. The architect here has gone from ensuring the safety of the building's inhabitants to engaging in defensive tactics, which could possibly increase the security of the occupants should the structure come under attack, or just as likely decrease it by making the structure a target.

Such an extreme case highlights a common dilemma in the production of architecture. The architect has a professional duty to accommodate the needs of a client as long as those programmatic requirements lie within the law and do not endanger occupants or passersby. At the same time, the architect has an obligation to protect people's health, safety, and welfare, even if they never know how the architect has done so. But does the architect also have an obligation to inform the inhabitants of a building about aspects of it that could endanger them? That certainly happens with signage that, for instance, warns people not to leave fire doors ajar, not to lean over railings in high-up locations, or not to access spaces that contain potentially hazardous materials. Such warnings constitute reasonable safety precautions intended

Figure 47.2 The military installations of the Cold War, with their radar domes and missile silos, have the same aesthetic as the minimalist and high-tech architecture of the time, with futuristic forms combined with utilitarian structures.

to protect people and most of us no doubt welcome such advice. However, there remain myriad examples of architects protecting people's safety that go unstated: preventing falls on stairs with slip-proof treads and readily accessible handrails, for example, or protecting against electrical shock with grounded outlets and switches.

Should an architect stay equally quiet about a less imminent and yet gravely serious threat, such as a missile attack? The client likely does not want to alarm or scare away tenants and the country, just as likely, might not want others to know of the installation, evident in the request that the architect disguise the missiles at the top of the building. But does an architect have a duty to inform people of the potential danger and the precautions taken to protect them? Utilitarian ethics can help answer such questions by asking: What constitutes the greatest good for the greatest number?

The citizens of the country certainly know of their hostile neighbors and of the possibility of missile attacks, so the architect has no need to inform them of that. But the architect does have an obligation to not only do as the client asks, but also to lay out the pros and cons of informing the building's occupants and to say what he or she would do in the case of an attack. While that might dissuade some from wanting to occupy the building, it might also lead others to choose it, since few buildings would have the same level of protection. Honesty isn't always the best course, especially if the goal is to mislead terrorists through distractions and smokescreens, but in the case of this building and its occupants, honesty is the safest – and most ethical – course of action.

Chapter 48

Trespassing

Of all the ethical issues related to the built environment, trespassing seems clear cut, being both against the law and obviously wrong. But the idea of "recreational trespass," as the UK geographer Bradley Garrett has documented, raises a number of questions about private property and public space that should give us pause, since the ethics of them are anything but clear (Garrett, 2012). Garrett has conducted ethnographic research into the large and dispersed community of recreational trespassers, people who explore construction sites and urban infrastructure typically off-limits to people not involved in their fabrication or maintenance, and who post photos of their exploits on the web to share with everyone else. While Garrett acknowledges the illegality of these activities, he also exposes the complex ethical dilemmas this reveals.

For example, why is so much of the infrastructure paid for by taxpayers off limits to the public that has funded it? The answer may seem obvious. Infrastructure that we all depend on needs to remain secure and inaccessible to those who might damage it and such systems also present safety hazards for people unequipped to navigate their potential dangers. And yet public servants and utility companies could make infrastructure open in other ways, virtually through digital video capture or physically through occasional guided tours, which would not only make it make available to more people than urban trespassers, but also discourage the latter from their illegal ventures by making the destinations more accessible and less mysterious. Garrett's work causes us to ask how much the breaking of rules stems from the unnecessarily restrictive nature of the rules themselves.

Recreational trespassers also have a lot to teach us about the more decrepit aspects of our built environment. Garrett notes how many consider themselves to be the "informal custodian(s) of derelict space," paying attention to places that no one else seems to notice or care for, something that cities have in ample supply. This, in turn, should lead us to ask why we have so much derelict space and what ethical obligations we have to maintain what others depend on, and what else underutilized space in our cities could be used for, especially for those who lack space or a home.

Figure 48.1 Most people find abandoned buildings alluring, perhaps in part because of their metaphorical role as a reminder of our own mortality, and as such, they need to be cared for as much as we would a dying person.

The answer again seems clear: the public sector has the right to determine, through zoning laws, who uses what land for what purpose and, through funding allocations, what infrastructure gets maintained and what does not.

That does not mean, though, that the public sector can or should do nothing about the underused or derelict space in its purview; it has an ethical responsibility to do so. Utilitarian ethics argues that the best course of action creates the greatest good for the greatest number, which suggests that when public officials or private property owners behave in ways that work against the good of the larger community, we all have the duty to act. Here, urban trespassers might have something to offer. Instead of the conflicts that can occur between the public and private sectors over the maintenance of their property, we could encourage the informal custodianship of derelict places, allowing people to pay attention to and even care for what others do not seem to care about.

Another motto of the recreational trespassing community, Garrett reports, is the idea that "everywhere is free space." While not true legally, such a statement begs the questions of what we mean by freedom and why we attach ownership to physical space, with trespassers causing us to doubt the usual answers we give to them. Our freedom gets framed not just by the laws we live under, but also by our willingness to take responsibility for our actions, as the existentialist Jean-Paul Sartre argued (Sartre, 1956). If everyone is free, in that existentialist sense, then everywhere is free as well, even if that means accepting the consequences of our actions, including our arrest for acting as if it is.

The idea of property rights has obvious value: it prompts us to take care of what we own and to protect it from those who would damage or destroy it. But what about recreational trespassers, who do no harm except to challenge the inviolate nature of property rights? By visiting off-limit spaces to experience and document it, they highlight the often-unfounded fear that underpins property and that rests on an assumption that others will take it or at least take advantage of it if we let down our guard. Perhaps we need a new tradition related to the stewardship of property, periodically opening up usually inaccessible places to neighbors, community members, and other respectful visitors, as happens with house tours and historic sites. This might make recreational trespassing obsolete or make us all fellow travelers.

If capitalistic economies depend upon the right of property, so too do they tend to produce a surplus of goods and spaces, which recreational trespassers also reveal in their adventures, often at night. We divide space not just in terms of ownership, but also in terms of time, with a lot of space remaining idle either over the course of the day or at night, depending upon its role, and trespassers underscore that fact through their off-hours forays. Their example suggests that we could occupy space more efficiently, with different uses depending upon the time of day, rather than have so much of it lying inactive so much of the time. Their trespasses also highlight the amount of resources we deploy in order to heat, light, or cool the empty spaces they tour, showing us through their exploits how we might all live more lightly, as visitors on this planet rather than its presumed masters.

Recreational trespassing also sheds light on the odd relationship architectural firms have with the buildings they design and see constructed. Urban explorers often gravitate to construction sites, finding ways past the perimeter fences and protective barriers that typically surround such places, and in this, they echo what architects do, observing construction in locations that the public isn't allowed. While construction administration has a different legal status than trespassing, there no doubt remains something of the same voyeuristic thrill that comes from seeing something not yet complete and still inaccessible to all but a few.

Here observation and surveillance intersect: whether we view something in an official capacity or watch out for people doing something unofficial, the intention behind that activity does not change the act of seeing itself. Getting us to see things in new ways, recreational trespassers have a role

Figure 48.2 Architects, engineers, and contractors have access to construction sites that recreational trespassers seek in order to experience them for themselves and bring that experience to the masses via photography online.

to play in getting us to rethink our use of space and resources in ways that should arrest us, even if we end up arresting them.

References

Garrett, Bradley. 2012. "Undertaking Recreational Trespass: Urban Exploration and Infiltration," *Transactions*. Institute of British Geographers, 39(1), August, 1–13.

Sartre, Jean-Paul. 1956. *Being and Nothingness*. New York: Philosophical Library.

Chapter 49

Value

When studying ethics in graduate school, I ran across two of my former architecture classmates who seemed confused by the path I had taken, away from the expected route of working in an architectural office toward something that, as one of them said, seemed so useless. I understood where that comment came from: in a field as tied to usefulness as architecture, ethics can seem theoretical or impractical. But I also wondered if their aversion to ethics had to do with its making some designers uncomfortable by raising sometimes-challenging questions about the design professions' complicity in reinforcing the privilege of some people over others. Among all the arts, this seems particularly an issue in architecture, which, because of its difficulty and expense, often finds itself accommodating and reinforcing the advantages of those who have the money to commission it. Ethics can also raise questions about how architecture not only creates the physical facades of buildings, but also the veneer of propriety that can cover up behavior on the part of those who commission a structure or inhabit it. Perhaps because of such questioning, ethics has not had the visibility or received the attention that it deserves, either in architectural education or in the discourse about our field – a point that I tried to make with my skeptical classmates so many years ago, without success.

Architecture arose as an organized profession in the United States in the second half of the nineteenth century, coinciding with a widespread effort, led by the critic Oscar Wilde, to separate the realm of aesthetics from that of ethics. We see that separation in the formalism and aestheticism of nineteenth- and early twentieth-century Beaux Arts architecture, in which the focus on the creation of classical facades and idealized interior and exterior environments papered over the industrial pollution, environmental destruction, and social inequality that enriched the public and private clients of those buildings.

Architects themselves played a somewhat paradoxical role in this. On one hand, the profession had become complicit in enabling those in power to feel good about themselves, with the discourse in schools of architecture largely focused on the skill with which students could learn this classical disguise. One the other hand, the profession itself found itself increasingly exploited

Figure 49.1 Beaux Arts architecture reflected the worthy desire of connecting to the ideas of the Roman Republic, and the unworthy one of ennobling those who held political or economic power at a time of great inequality.

by those in power, which led, in 1909, to the AIA's first code of ethics. The prohibitions in that first code against the exploitative practices of clients wanting architects, for example, to give away their design ideas in unpaid competitions or to compete for work based on who had the lowest fees, shows how much the unfair treatment that had enriched those who commissioned buildings had gotten applied to those who designed them.

The rise of modern architecture in the 1920s and 30s might seem like a ripping away of the Beaux Arts façade and the recognition of the needs of the working class. Modern architects' admiration of industrial architecture, their emphasis on transparency, and their attention to new kinds of programs, such as worker housing, all reinforced that appearance. But modern architecture actually represented a new kind of ethical slight-of-hand, based on what the philosopher William Barrett has called "the illusion of technique" (Barrett, 1978). While modern architecture seemed more sympathetic to the plight of the working class through the use of industrial materials and methods, the profession and the schools did little to challenge the social, economic or political power of clients. In addition, the International

Style that characterized so much of early modernist architecture ignored differences of culture or climate, turning the idea of universal rights into a form of repression.

Ethics finally emerged in the late 1960s as an explicit area of study in architectural education, becoming part of the accreditation process in the 1970s. Since then, we have seen a flourishing of ethical questioning in our field: challenges to the dominance of men and male ways of thinking on the part of feminist ethics, challenges to the dominance of humans over other species on the part of environmental ethics, challenges to the dominance of capitalism and its exploitation of workers on the part of Marxist ethics, or challenges to the dominance of reason and abstract rationality on the part of phenomenological ethics. That ethical turn in architecture education has greatly enriched the intellectual life in our discipline. It has also sensitized the profession to the impact of our decisions, actions, and behavior on others, especially those without wealth and power to commission our work, giving rise to public-interest design and system design as new sub-fields within the design professions.

At the same time, we have seen a resurgence in aestheticism and the illusion of technique as a result of the digital revolution, in which computer-generated form-making and digital fabrication methods have become an end in themselves, with the needs of the global population, future generations, and other species on the planet largely overlooked. This apparent turn away from ethics has a conservative character and paradoxically so, given the Avant Garde nature of digitally-based form-making. By treating architecture as a kind of object divorced from its social and spatial context, and by focusing on the process of its making rather than on the implications of what is made, digital fabrication often implicitly accepts the status quo, despite the radical self-image. What we chose to ignore says far more about us than we chose to address and ignoring equity or sustainability in favor of inventive forms and efficient form-making speaks volumes.

This also reflects an old tension between aesthetics and ethics. Both have conceptions of what constitutes the good and yet we still seem to divide ourselves based on how we make those judgments: visually and spatially on one hand, and intellectually and conceptually on the other. That, of course, remains a false division; the visual and spatial have an intellectual and conceptual component and vice versa. But the retreat from ethics on the part of some in architectural circles has put a new spin on that old debate by viewing digital fabrication as an end in itself and not a means to some other, ethical end. In some cases, this gets framed as a difference between basic research – the making of objects based on algorithms regardless of their function – and applied research, with the latter portrayed as a kind of philistine interference with the pursuit of knowledge for its own sake. In other cases, digital fabrication becomes aligned with the engineering and scientific disciplines as opposed to the arts and humanities, with their questions about value and meaning that seem outside the bounds of a purely technical path.

Figure 49.2 This thermoformed bus shelter by Associated Fabrication for the 2010 Winter Olympics shows how digital fabrication can align ethics and aesthetics, creating low-cost and elegant shelter for people of all means.

The polarization of the digital and the ethical in architecture, like that in our politics, misses the real opportunities of finding common ground and complementary purpose. Globally, the greatest need for architecture exists among the billions of poorly housed people on the planet, for whom low-cost, modestly sized, and efficiently operated shelter remains a largely unfulfilled need, and for which digital fabrication has an answer. The latter's ability to rapidly produce shelter and furnishings, near to where the need remains the greatest, represents an enormous advance and one that highlights the relationship between our digital capacity and our ethical responsibility. As a professor of mine liked to remind us in graduate school, the word aesthetics has the letters for the word ethics within it and the two are much stronger together than apart.

Reference

Barrett, William. 1978. *The Illusion of Technique: A Search for Meaning in a Technological Civilization*. New York: Anchor Books.

Chapter 50

Work

I had a professor once say that a good life, a happy one, comes from aligning our vocation with our avocation, finding ways to get paid for what we love to do and would do anyway, whether or not we got compensated for it. I have tried to follow that advice, with mixed success. I have had jobs that seemed perfect aligned with my interests, but that had other problems, such as unpleasant or overly demanding bosses, who made it not worth the effort. Still, I have found that if we are willing to live within our means and accept the pay level that our skills command in the marketplace, plenty of vocations exist for every avocation. It's a matter of finding work that seems less like work and more like play.

That may sound overly idealistic, especially to those who work in unfulfilling jobs in order to support what they really love to do in their evenings, weekends, and holidays. But that professor's comment highlights a peculiar feature of the modern world that Hannah Arendt identified in her book, *The Human Condition*. She made a distinction between the craft-oriented work of our hands and the commodity-focused work of our bodies, arguing that the modern world has made us less expressive fabricators – *homo faber* – and more like oppressed laborers – *animal laborans* (Arendt, 1958, p. 199).

Although I didn't know of Arendt's writing at the time, I went into architecture in part because I saw, in my grandfather architect, someone whose vocation and avocation were the same. This had its downsides, since he worked seven days a week and went to work every day until well past his 100th year, not because he had to work, but because he wanted to. Although he might have tempered his enthusiasm for work somewhat, which might have saved his first marriage, for instance, his love for what he did seemed to me an ideal way of living.

I also saw, though, architects who did not see it that way. In one office I worked in, some of the partners and staff complained a lot about the long hours and the time it took away from other things they wanted to do: fishing in one case, painting in another. That experience taught me that even an avocation-oriented vocation does not work for everyone and that maybe those complainers should have become professional fishermen

Figure 50.1 An architect who worked from the age of 16 to 101 designing buildings, my grandfather never separated vocation and advocation, always looking ahead to the next project. Here at the office exploring the next idea.

or artists. I decided then and there that I would only do what I had a hard time stopping when I was tired and couldn't wait to get back to when I awoke. Luck and privilege have had some role in my being able to do so much of the time since then, but I also think such a life lies in wait for anyone who chooses to follow it. Kant argued that we should do the right thing regardless of the consequences and that applies to ourselves and our own lives as well as our behavior toward others (Kant, 2016).

Kant's maxim may become even more relevant in the years ahead as work itself begins to change in some dramatic ways. Arendt saw how fulfilling work had become repetitive drudgery in the modern era, but she did not live to see a time, like now, in which machines have not only enhanced human labor, but also begun to replace it. As Carl Frey and Michael Osborne at the University of Oxford have shown, we face the prospect of almost 50% of current jobs becoming susceptible to automation in the coming years (Frey and Osborne, 2013), especially jobs that involve repetitive, predictable, or dangerous work, which computers and robots can do better, faster, and cheaper than most humans. The number of jobs available to us will likely shrink and the nature of work will certainly change, which leads to the question of what will replace the many blue-collar and white-collar vocations that get automated.

One answer: avocations. When you look at the work that resists automation, they tend to cluster in one of six areas, which I will call the "six Cs," which people do better than the most advanced computers or robots and probably always will. The first involve Caring jobs, which range from raising or teaching of children to attending to the elderly or healing the sick. The second: Communication jobs, which involve everything from sales and marketing to litigation and negotiation. The third: Craft jobs, which span from the skilled making of things to the providing of services of all sorts. The fourth: Construction jobs, which require dexterity and involve complexities that robots may never master. The fifth: Creative jobs, which engage our imagination every time we generate something that hasn't been thought or done before. And the sixth: Community jobs, which focus on connecting citizens, leveraging local assets, and creating opportunities for the people of a place.

Arendt would have applauded the coming of an economy that revolved around caring, communication, craft, construction, creativity, and community.

THE MANOR HOUSE, KELMSCOTT, FROM THE FARM.

Figure 50.2 William Morris, in *News from Nowhere*, envisioned a future in which people worked as they did before the industrial revolution, doing what we are good at and what machines are not: an idea whose time has come.

Such jobs recall the kind of work that people did before the industrial revolution, and they indicate a movement away from the *animal laborans* of the modern age and back toward the *homo faber* that defined the premodern work world and seems likely to define the postmodern one as well. Some the "six Cs" will involve handcraft and human interactions that may not look much different from what pre-industrial people did and have always done. Much of it, though, will likely use automation to complement the work that needs doing, much as architects do now, with computers enhancing the ability to design in more creative, constructive, and craft-like ways.

The "six C" jobs also relate closely to what many people now do as avocations, be it caring for children, communicating ideas, crafting products, constructing places, connecting people, or creating something new. Our avocations, in other words, hold the key for our future vocations and the alignment of the two becomes not some idealistic dream, but the most practical of tasks, as we create new jobs from what we are already good at, with skills that no computer or robot can match. The transition from *animal laborans* back to *homo faber* will represent a huge challenge, given the number of jobs that will disappear and the number of workers displaced as a result, which is why we need to start now in educating children to get ready for "six C" work and in retraining adults for the new jobs that await them. The disruption, though, will be worth it in the end. No one wants to do repetitive or dangerous work, and the automation of those jobs will free us all to do what we most love to do and can't wait to do. This represents an enormous step forward to what humans used to do so well and a real advance in what Arendt called the human condition, which will always remain at the core of both architecture and ethics.

References

Arendt, Hannah. 1958. *The Human Condition.* Chicago: University of Chicago Press.
Frey, Carl Benedikt & Osborne, Michael A. 2013. *The Future of Employment: How Susceptible are Jobs to Computerization?* Oxford: Oxford Martin School.
Kant, Immanuel. 2016. *The Collected Works of Immanuel Kant.* London: Delphi Classics.
Morris, William. 2009. *News from Nowhere.* Oxford: Oxford University Press.

Epilogue
A theory of architecture and ethics

I feel an obligation, at the conclusion of this book, to try to condense these diverse essays into a more concise and coherent theory about the relationship of architecture and ethics. While much of what follows has already appeared in various places and in different ways in this book, I thought it might be useful to have it stated in one place and as simply as possible.

With that in mind, I will begin with some assumptions: Except for those who might have some sort of sociopathic or masochistic personality disorder, all of us – as deontological ethics claims – have a basic grasp of right and wrong, which we learn growing up in various social situations and which we continue to relearn as we go through life. Most people – as Aristotle argued – also understand the merits of such virtues as fairness, courage, temperance, and prudence, which we acquire as well by watching and interacting with others and by observing what happens when those virtues don't exist. That extends to our sense of what constitutes a good society, one that also values these traits and that embeds them into the public policies and legal structure of a country or community. Some cultures may stress some values and some virtues over others, but as moral foundationalists argue, those differences are more a matter of emphasis than of any fundamental disagreement.

Which leads to the question: If there exists such widespread understanding of, and general agreement about, what constitutes right and wrong, why does so much unethical behavior still occur? I would answer that question as follows:

> Unethical behavior arises from a spatial and temporal disconnect between our actions and their consequences, a disconnect that can blind us to the potentially negative effect of what we do because its impacts frequently occur in some far-off place or unknown future. Likewise, ethical behavior stems from an understanding of its consequences not only on others in our immediate sphere, but also on distant populations, future generations, and other species.

In short, people do bad things because they think they can get away with it, and while we may be an intelligent species, we are also a self-interested and short-sighted one.

This consequentialist argument runs up against the criticism that we cannot know the full effects of our actions on others in some distant land nor do we know what will happen in the future, and so making that a criterion for judging ethical or unethical behavior seems impractical if not impossible. As finite human beings, we all suffer from a spatial and temporal disconnect from others not in our immediate lives, and so that disconnection cannot be a driver of unethical behavior or we would all behave that way. Which is my point. Unethical behavior is far more common than we might think, given what we know about right and wrong, because of the limitations of our spatial and temporal imagination, making us unable – or unwilling – to contemplate what impact a decision or action might have on those spatially or temporally distant from ourselves.

Which is where architecture comes into play. Among all the other things that buildings do for us – such as keeping us warm, ensuring our privacy, and fending off the rain – they also connect us spatially and temporally. We spend most of our time in buildings, interacting with others in the spaces – the rooms and corridors – provided for our use, and we do so over time, be it an hour, a day, or a lifetime. As such, architecture shows us how our actions here and now can affect others who might use the same spaces at some future point, even if we do not know them or will never see them.

Architecture arises out of a design process that also helps us imagine the impacts of our choices. Buildings use materials and products from all over the world, made by people most of us will never meet, and yet these items affect us every day in the structures we use, giving us a direct spatial connection to far-off places and an opportunity to imagine the hands that mined the material or manufactured the product. Buildings also give us a temporal connection to those who came before us, in existing buildings or with handed-down objects, as well as to those who will follow us, occupying the spaces we do and perhaps using them in different ways. Design, in other words, instills in us an ethical habit of mind, as Aristotle might call it: one that involves balancing various factors in making decisions and imagining the spatial and temporal impacts of what we do.

A skeptic might argue at this point that people have long designed and occupied buildings and that has not stopped them from acting unethically. In fact, as mentioned in this book, some of the most unethical people of our time are involved in the construction of buildings. To this, I would counter with John Rawls's idea of the veil of ignorance. Rawls used that idea to guide decision-making by supposing that none of the decision-makers in a room knew their current situation. Since we all do know our status at the moment, his idea was mainly a useful thought experiment. But we do all live behind a veil of ignorance when it comes to the effects of our decisions or actions not only on distant populations, but also on ourselves in the near future. Those who engage in moral hazard may try to do all they can to avoid an unexpected setback, but no one can know what the future will bring or what we bring upon ourselves when we treat others unfairly.

So, let me end with another thought experiment: imagine the building that you now occupy as the entire world. Were that true, you would almost certainly make decisions and take actions that would not negatively effect on the others who occupy that same building and who you cannot avoid, since that building is all there is. You now depend upon them as your only community and you would not want to damage your relationship with them nor your reputation among them. In other words, when spatially and temporally connected to the people who lives we affect, only the most self-destructive person would behave badly toward them, since the most negative impacts of all would accrue to the person who acted unethically.

In some sense, that thought experiment has become a reality in the era of the Internet and the Internet-of-Things. We have shrunk space and time so dramatically through our digital connections that we can no longer escape the consequences of our actions: the earth has always been our home, our "eco," but it now exists, at least conceptually, at the scale of our actual homes, in which no deed or decision goes unnoticed for very long. Terrestrial space has become like architectural space, in which thriving depends upon our anticipating the effects of what we do now and into the future on those with whom we share this home, this microcosm that we call earth.

Index